Practical
TEACHING
Methods K-6

It's not what you look at that matters; it's what you see.

—Henry David Thoreau

Practical
TEACHING
Methods K-6

Sparking the Flame of Learning

Pamela Fannin Wilkinson

Margaret A. McNutt

Esther S. Friedman

CORWIN PRESS, INC.
A Sage Publications Company
Thousand Oaks, California

For information:

Corwin Press, Inc.
A Sage Publications Company
2455 Teller Road
Thousand Oaks, California 91320
www.corwinpress.com

Sage Publications Ltd.
6 Bonhill Street
London EC2A 4PU
United Kingdom

Sage Publications India Pvt. Ltd.
B-42 Panchsheel Enclave
Post Box 4109
New Delhi 110 017 India

Printed in the United States of America

Library of Congress Cataloging-in-Publication Data

Wilkinson, Pamela Fannin.
Practical teaching methods, K-6 : sparking the flame of learning / Pamela Fannin Wilkinson, Margaret A. McNutt, Esther S. Friedman.
    p. cm.
ISBN 0-7619-4602-0 (cloth) — ISBN 0-7619-4603-9 (pbk.)
    1. Elementary school teaching—United States. 2. Education, Elementary—United States—Curricula. I. McNutt, Margaret A. II. Friedman, Esther S. III. Title.
LB1570 .W576 2003
372.1102—dc21

2002151359

This book is printed on acid-free paper.

02   03   04   05   06   07   7   6   5   4   3   2   1

Acquisitions Editor:	Faye Zucker
Editor at Large:	Mark F. Goldberg
Editorial Assistant:	Julia Parnell
Production Editor:	Olivia Weber
Typesetter:	C&M Digitals (P) Ltd
Indexer:	Michael Ferreira
Cover Designer:	Michael Dubowe
Production Artist:	Sandra Ng Sauvajot

Contents

Acknowledgments

The authors are indebted to our own teachers and to those who let us work in their classrooms. We appreciate the support and encouragement of our families and friends. We dedicate this book to all who spark the flame of learning.

Corwin Press gratefully acknowledges the contributions of the following reviewers:

Douglas Llewellyn
Director of Science
Rochester City Schools
Rochester, NY

Ann Lambros
Center for Excellence in Research, Teaching, and Learning
    (CERTL)
Winston-Salem, NC

Michelle Collay
School Coach
Bay Area Coalition for Equitable Schools
Oakland, CA

Susan Drake
Brock University
Faculty of Education
St. Catharine's
Ontario, Canada

Jon Hinojosa
Executive Director
Say Sí
San Antonio, TX

Sandra Lynn Satterwhite
Educational Consultant
Charter School Specialist
Houston, TX

About the Authors

Pamela Fannin Wilkinson is a writer, teacher, and consultant for education and business with more than 20 years of experience. She served as an Artist-in-Education under Texas Commission on the Arts and publishes regularly. Pam develops programs for public and private schools, as well as for businesses. She holds a Bachelor of Science degree in Education from Southwestern University, Georgetown, Texas.

Margaret A. McNutt has over 20 years of experience in both public and private education at all grade levels. Her roles include classroom teacher, administrator, curriculum developer, and technology designer.

Margaret serves as a consultant to schools regarding staff development, student achievement in all subject areas, and technology design. Margaret holds a Bachelor of Arts degree in English and a Master of Arts degree in Education from Austin College, Sherman, Texas. She is a candidate for a Ph.D. in English from the University of Houston.

Esther S. Friedman has extensive experience as teacher, school administrator, program developer, and trainer for both parent and teacher groups in public and private settings. She has served in organizations at the national, state, and local level.

Esther holds a Bachelor of Arts degree in Education from State University of New York at Potsdam and a Master of Library Science degree in School Library and Media from the University of Oklahoma. She is a candidate for an Ed.D. in Curriculum and Instruction from the University of Houston.

CORWIN PRESS

The Corwin Press logo—a raven striding across an open book—represents the happy union of courage and learning. We are a professional-level publisher of books and journals for K-12 educators, and we are committed to creating and providing resources that embody these qualities. Corwin's motto is "Success for All Learners."

CHAPTER ONE

The Premise

Necessity is the mother of taking chances.

—Mark Twain (1872)

WHY DID WE WRITE THIS BOOK?

As educators with more than 60 years of experience among us, we enjoy seeing and working with students, teachers, administrators, parents, and all the other people who help to make a school what it is. We have taught, consulted with schools, and made workshop presentations; and two of us served for many years as elementary principals. We also delight in the various subjects and in watching, helping, and encouraging students to learn.

This book examines many of the best practices and methods for each curricular area as established in national norms. Some of our suggestions are similar to those made by well-informed educators 40 years ago, but many are based on practices that emerged in the last 20 years and have worked in hundreds and, in some cases, thousands of classrooms across the country.

WHO SHOULD READ THIS BOOK?

This book is designed primarily for teachers and administrators of students in kindergarten through Grade 6 who wish to examine where they are and where they might go. The format allows educators to use single chapters to concentrate on a particular subject area or to use the entire book as a professional-development tool that can renew, reenergize, and reinvigorate teaching practices for individuals or for a school's faculty as a whole.

We focus on all the major content areas in an elementary school: the strands of language and their relationship to language development and critical thinking, mathematics, science, social studies, technology, the library media center, and the arts (which include movement and physical education). We address professional growth and the need to keep teachers' curiosity alive despite pressing schedules and responsibilities. We acknowledge the difficulties faced daily by many teachers, working under circumstances where schools are understaffed and underserved; but rather than offering still another analysis of school reform and governance, we choose instead to focus on instructional strengths such as the dynamic that emerges when thoughtful and curious teachers guide attentive and curious students.

In our current work as consultants, we sometimes encounter teachers who don't enjoy students as much as they once did, administrators who have diminished appreciation for their teachers, and parents who are either confused by the system or who hold educators in low regard. Teachers and administrators frequently feel their jobs and self-esteem are threatened by an accountability system which seems to hold them responsible for all the woes of the world; and some parents disapprove of classrooms which are unlike those in which they grew up and of a system which seems not to be doing enough for their children.

We accept that schools must be accountable but not that accountability requires us to relinquish those practices that make teaching enjoyable and creative and make learning enjoyable and continuous. No accountability system should work against serious learning and genuine enthusiasm for teaching and learning. The wonderful thing about effective teaching based on what really works for teachers and students is that both enthusiasm for school and test scores rise.

HOW IS THE BOOK DESIGNED?

Standards

National standards are the foundation for textbooks and local mandates. It is an impossible task to track or address all of these separately as they multiply and change, district by district, state by state, across educational communities. However, the use of national standards provides a consistent framework for each of the content areas, and examples throughout this book demonstrate practical applications of those norms in the elementary classroom.

Curriculum

In each chapter, we discuss the elements of a good program for the area under consideration. We provide real examples from real schools with ideas that work, along with our reflections regarding these examples, and assessment tips. Finally, we provide a list of resources that may be used by the classroom teacher. Again, readers will find some of the material quite familiar and some new. What is original is that educators now have one clear handbook that covers virtually all the curricular areas in Grades K-6.

Creative Teaching

We intend for this work to be used as a guide for the elementary classroom teacher, K-6, although we know that many of the concepts and practices work well in grades beyond. We believe that both new and seasoned professionals will find themselves capable of the practices discussed and described; and we think that such methods will spark the flame of learning.

RESOURCE

Twain, Mark. (1872) *Roughing It.* Retrieved July 27, 2002, from www. twainquotes.com/Necessity.html

Writers Are Readers and Thinkers, Too

I hear and I forget. I see and I remember. I do and I understand.

—Chinese Proverb

LANGUAGE STRANDS

Language is the currency of classroom exchange, and a strong language arts program emphasizes the four language strands—reading, writing, listening, and speaking. Each strand is equally important to the whole, and each is enmeshed throughout the process employed to write. A reliable program, one that becomes the foundation for learning, is based more on method than on the use of prescribed materials. You and your students will discover a wealth of material by examining your own interests and pursuing them as the core for assignments.

The permeation of language across the curriculum provides continuity for your writing projects. By focusing on text in its infinite expression and form, you broaden interest in all the content areas. By adapting a variety of sources and applications, you stimulate imagination daily. Reading, speaking, and listening become the basis for writing, which is integral to all subject areas.

READING

How to teach reading is the most heavily emphasized area in elementary-teacher preparation. Without debating or restating the merits of particular programs, we want simply to list in summary form the findings released by the National Reading Panel (2000). According to the panel, students must be taught the following in order to be good readers:

1. *Phonemic awareness skills*—the ability to manipulate the sounds that make up spoken language

2. *Phonics skills*—the understanding that there are relationships between letters and sounds

3. *Reading fluency*—the ability to read with accuracy, speed, and expression

4. *Comprehension*—the skills required to apply reading comprehension strategies to enhance understanding and enjoyment of what they read

The panel also found that the most effective reading instruction includes a combination of methods. Students should enjoy reading, should read good materials, and should learn a range of skills to interpret what they read. This means that phonics, whole language, guided reading (both silent and oral), and a variety of reading comprehension strategies, including listening and speaking, are necessary.

Because writing is the synthesis of all the language strands, this chapter focuses primarily on the writing process.

WRITING

Writing—the word often strikes fear in the hearts of young and old alike because many of us have had tough experiences with writing at one time or another. Writing—whether learning it or teaching it—is hard work. Good writing requires continual improvement and work: searching for ideas; proofreading and revising; vocabulary development; logical thought processes;

knowledge of punctuation, capitalization, syntax, and sentence structure; and on and on and on. And all this requires time, lots of time. Why wouldn't we be afraid?

But we cannot permit fear or lack of time to stop us from teaching students to write well, because learning to write well contributes to so many other things. It enhances the ability to think critically. Writing crosses the boundaries of subject matter. It is not something that happens only in language arts or English class. Writing is part of science and social studies and every other school subject and of real-world work. Once students understand the process involved in good writing, they have opened possibilities in all areas.

The Writing Process

Humans are naturally curious, driven both to build and to take apart, to create as well as understand what makes things work. The exercise of language, and of writing in particular, offers rich exploration of these desires.

The steps of the writing process have been well documented and detailed since the publication of results from the National Writing Project (2002) in the 1980s and 1990s. In quick review, those steps or stages are the following:

- Prewriting
- Drafting
- Responding and revising
- Proofreading and editing
- Publishing
- Assessment

While most teachers are aware of these steps, implementation in the classroom remains problematic. Following are some strategies to ease implementation.

Stage I: Prewriting

Prewriting includes all the activities that you and your students do before formal writing actually begins. Word games and associations, brainstorming and discussion, mapping and webbing—all of these constitute prewriting, as do the reading and discussion of related poems, articles from newspapers or periodicals, or other materials that illuminate the work at hand. Prewriting establishes focus and elicits matter for consideration. To write, students need to have words, pictures, topics, or other materials that are the basis for their writing and give them a reason to write. This holds for sentences, poems, paragraphs, stories, reports, longer papers—any writing your students do.

At first, short sessions are more effective than a single long one. For students in Grades 1 or 2 or those less experienced in writing, start with 10 or 15 minutes a day for each of 3 or 4 successive days before composing. These intervals should be linked thematically. Listening to music and discussing a photograph, a piece of pottery or statuary, a painting, or thought for the day make potential links. Each contributes to information gathering and organization before writing starts.

Do all you can to create an interest in language and ideas. The first step is to get students interested in writing and to give them the words and prompts they'll need to get started. Choose materials that suit your interests and those of your students to use as prompts. At the end of this chapter in Resources, we suggest books that we have found helpful, but any textbook or work—fiction, nonfiction, poems, songs, advertisements, newspaper or magazine articles, books, and other sources will do.

Prewriting may occur in response to a prompt, or a topic can arise out of the activities themselves. Prewriting can be whole-group, small-group, paired, or individual work.

Prompts: Ready to Write

When introducing a writing prompt, give students a good explanation of what is expected and how they will be helped to complete the assignment. Begin by discussing the purpose and the outcome of the writing. Discuss the components of the writing and reassure students that their ideas will take form and shape as they move through the stages of the writing process.

For example, if primary students are going to write about animals, tell them they will see pictures of five animals and will list things they know about one animal of their choice (dog, elephant, lion, cat, cow). The assignment will be to write three sentences about that animal. They might begin this alone or in small groups. The teacher could even do an example of a sixth animal with the whole class. The teacher should list the steps of the process on the chalkboard or an overhead and reassure the students they will get help with each step.

In the following three examples of prewriting, different prompts are presented and discussed. The first uses a picture book to explore perspective and point of view, while the second and third use poetry and music respectively.

Example 1: Prewriting—Working With Perspective

Seeing the ordinary in an unusual way widens point of view. For instance, *Numblers*, a picture book by Suse MacDonald and Bill Oakes, manipulates the shapes and positions of numerals to create art. This book can be used as a prompt to help students gain perspective at any elementary grade level. By perspective, we mean the ability to see things from more than one point of view. After looking at the book together and discussing what we see (and how we see it as led by the book's authors), each student chooses a number between 1 and 100. Students then write their number on a piece of unlined paper and, without any erasures, incorporate that number into a picture or design.

While creating their artwork, students also make a word bank in a corner of the page so that a story or idea will emerge. Together, picture and words become individualized prompts that can lead to a story. (See Chapter 3 for a detailed lesson.)

Example 2: Prewriting—Exploring Color

Another method to get started is to use poetry to spark imagination. Mary O'Neill's *Hailstones and Halibut Bones* is a true favorite among many students. The book itself is an exploration of color personifications in the form of poems. Imaginative illustrations accompany each poem. Students enjoy exploring the nuances of color needed for precise description. Further, with teacher-led discussion, ideas from the poems tend to fall into large categories, which may then be used to get students started on a piece of writing.

Selections from *Hailstones* are read to a fourth-grade class. Following students' comments and response, the group discusses favorite colors. Then every color noted is placed on the board; the class by majority chooses one color (perhaps red) that they as a group will write about. Next, each student is asked to contribute favorite red things. Most of the "red things" (in this instance) are kinds or items of food, which are categorized and fashioned into a poem. Finally, here is the group poem from Gail McGinnis's fourth-grade class in Houston, Texas:

Red

Red is the color of cherries, strawberries,
and tomatoes in the spring.
Watermelon is ripe in the summer.
Apples and pears are ripe in the fall.

Shrimp, crabs, and lobsters require Louisiana hot sauce.
Red snacks are hot Cheetos, snow cones, and
pizza with pepperoni—
make me thirsty for punch.

Now let's have a party with red velvet cake and balloons!

You can lead students into individual work by following the same steps. Invite them to close their eyes (the better to visualize) while you read chosen selections aloud. Discuss and brainstorm what happened—What pictures did you see? Why? Have each student choose a color, focus on the color (by starting with a list of things of that color), and write about it.

Students of all ages respond to this approach, even K-1 students who dictate what they have to say. The following examples demonstrate a progression between Grades 1 and 4. The first example was written after a first-grade science lesson.

The magma is red and hot. It finds a hole in the ground.
The mercury on the thermometer is red and shows you it is hot.
The lava is red and hot. It blows out lava and ash and rocks.

—Marvin, Grade 1, MacArthur
Elementary School, Houston, Texas

This poem exhibits nuance of color and expression:

A frog is the color of money.
A uniform is the color of the army.
A grasshopper is the color of grass.
A toad is the color of a green ivy plant.
A green rock is the color of an emerald earring.

—Alan, Grade 4,
Grissom Elementary, Houston, Texas

Having gone through this process and written color poems, sixth graders at Redbridge Middle School, Houston, Texas, wrote essays about why they liked the assignment. The following paragraph is a draft from one essay.

The Assignment I Most Enjoyed (rough draft)

In writing workshop, my class and I have had many assignments to work on. However, I have one favorite assignment, it was to write a poem about my favorite color. Manley, I enjoyed this assignment because the directions included ~~writing~~ my two favorite things, writing a poem and drawing a picture. ~~I also~~

—Caitlyn Flowers, Grade 6,
Redbridge Middle School, Houston, Texas

Example 3: Prewriting—Using Music

Music also works well as a writing prompt. Study songs as poems set to music, or look at the ballad as a way of spreading the news before the advent of newspapers. Many literature textbooks include ballads in the poetry section. For example, practically every country and western song is a ballad; it tells a story. A well-known country song is Charlie Daniels' "The Devil Went Down to Georgia." Students easily hear the uses of dialogue, both in the words of the song and in the interplay of instruments.

If you want melody to provide structure for writing, choose music without words—instrumental work. Play the piece first just for listening, then discuss mood and tone. Brainstorm words descriptive of the music. After more discussion, students develop descriptive paragraphs or poems.

As another example, Scott Joplin's "Pineapple Rag" from the movie soundtrack of *The Sting* illustrates unity of theme when one instrument sets the theme as all other instruments join the melody. Or choose a piece that has an easily heard dramatic shift. "Roll in the Tire" from the movie soundtrack of *To Kill a Mockingbird* (Bernstein) works very well here. Have students listen, then write a story based on the structure (mood, tone, and tempo) of the music.

If you want to demonstrate similarity of image, choose a group of related pieces where mood, tone, and tempo are consistent. Many teachers and students have music boxes that can be used for this. Students write poems (individual or group) patterned on the five senses. The poems express comparisons by using simile. Here is an example:

The music sounds like the wind blowing;
The music sounds like raindrops;
The music sounds like snowflakes falling from the sky.

The music looks like dolphins jumping from the sea.
The music looks like hearts flying everywhere.
The music smells like fresh roses in a garden.
The music tastes like chocolate ice cream with a cherry on top.
The music feels like two people with happiness and love coming
    into their lives.

—Writers' Camp Group Poem, by fourth, fifth, and sixth
graders, Grissom Elementary School, Houston, Texas

Stage II: Drafting

Before students begin to write, they must review their information from the prewriting lessons. Ideas can be listed in some logical sequence, and students should concentrate on getting all their ideas on paper in the first draft. Spelling, punctuation, and grammar are not the issue at this time; ideas are. Students often worry that the draft isn't perfect. They may stop and start and stop without getting a draft completed if they do not like messy work. Encourage them to push through to the end—that is, to get the ideas on paper so they can be shaped in the next step. Some teachers refer to the first draft as the "sloppy copy"; and it does seem to help some students realize that getting the writing down on paper is important at this stage, and careful shaping can wait until later.

One way to encourage and demonstrate the practice of drafting is to write together as a class. Use a flip chart, chalkboard, or overhead projector—the larger the better so that everyone can follow the flow of the piece. The teacher or a student writes sentences and paragraphs as they are constructed by the group, taking time to discuss, revise, and rewrite in the process but not erasing and starting over, simply marking and drawing arrows in this sloppy copy. This helps students to see how a first draft emerges. Following is a first draft done in Hector Amaya's bilingual third-grade class, written in response to a science lesson on rain.

I like the rain because <u>it make plant grow.</u>
What makes it great is <u>fresh water</u>.
The rain makes <u>streets wet</u>.
The rain sounds like <u>marbols foling</u>.
The rain smells like <u>baby</u>.
I like the rain because <u>you get wet</u>.

—Jessica Rivera, Bilingual Grade 3,
Grissom Elementary School, Houston, Texas

Stage III: Responding and Revising

Once the first draft is written, the student reads over the work, individually or with a partner. Through this step, the writer begins to hear and to evaluate the piece; to check information, organization, and language; to consider audience and purpose. Now the writer becomes both reader and listener. Students often hear more clearly what they have written if they read their work aloud or have someone read it to them. Is this what I mean to say? Have I said it clearly? Does this work instead?

Often, students profit from suggestions made by several other students if the teacher has set up writing groups of four to six students. Now punctuation, spelling, grammar, careful organization, the right word, and other conventions matter. See Box 2.1 for a fourth-grade paragraph-planning page and first and second drafts.

Stage IV: Proofreading and Editing

Now even more careful revisions are made. Errors in capitalization, punctuation, grammar, and spelling are marked and corrected. If students have access to computers with spell check and grammar check, these can be helpful as long as they understand the shortcomings of such programs. For example, spell check does not know the difference between *there, their,* and *they're* or *to, too,* and *two* or . . . well, you get the idea.

Depending on the student's level of expertise, this work can be done with classmate partners or with the teacher. Students can

> ### Box 2.1   Planning Page and Two Drafts, Grade 4, JeMarcus Thomas, Frost Elementary School, Houston, Texas
>
> #### Plaining Page
>
> Intro: Once upon a time I wen to Astroworld. I rode rides. I had a great time.
> Event 1: I rode Exciting rides
> Event 2: I rode scary rides
> Event 3: I rode Boring rides
> Con. When we got thrue we went to cicis pizza. Then I wrote in my jurnal I had a great time
>
> #### First Draft
>
> Astroworld
> When I went to Astroworld. I was excited. I rode ~~E~~xciting rides, ~~B~~oring rides and scacy rodes. I still had a good time. Let me tell you what happened on the ~~Exciting~~ rides!!
>
> #### Second Draft
>
> Astrworld
> When I went to Astroworld I was excited. I rode exciting, scary, and boring rides. I still had a good time. Let me tell you what happened on the all of the rides.

use any sources in the room that will help: age-appropriate dictionaries or a thesaurus; teaching assistant, classroom volunteer, or older student; information from earlier lessons on paragraphing or quotation marks. In this stage, the student shapes the piece as well as that student can.

Stage V: Publishing

When the piece is cleanly produced in final copy and ready for an audience beyond the writer, it can be considered as published. Access to computers and photocopying machines will produce a more professional appearance but is not required. Drawings or other artwork or decoration are often part of the finished work.

Following are ideas for presenting published work:

- *Individual books.* Students produce finished copies of several pieces of work, which are bound or collected as personal classroom books.
- *Illustrated manuscripts.* Once students produce a finished copy of their work, they are encouraged to illustrate the piece with relevant borders. Illuminated manuscripts from the Middle Ages are used as patterns for many contemporary picture book illustrations. This concept, using an ornate first letter of the text and borders incorporating details from the text, can be integrated into student work when a quote from a text is chosen and then illustrated.
- *Class anthologies.* Finished pieces from all students are illustrated, collected, reproduced, and bound for each student.
- *Class newspapers or newsletters.* Students write about themselves, their school, and other activities of interest. Periodically, pieces are formatted and produced for the larger school audience.
- *Collage of student work.* Using large rolls of paper, mount finished student writing for display.

Stage VI: Assessment

For writing assessment, the first thing to keep in mind is that every written piece does not have to be formally graded. Students can sometimes be evaluated according to criteria based on their participation and involvement in each step of the process. When you do wish to grade students, an evaluation form can help. That way both you and your students know exactly what is expected. The guidelines are given to students and discussed at a very early stage of writing.

See Figure 2.1 and Form 2.2 for evaluation criteria; suggestions for use have been noted on each. Form 2.1 provides some examples of integrated elements and assessment tips for writers who are readers and thinkers, too. Keep in mind that there are at least hundreds of assignments and prompts teachers could give students, and these forms are not intended to be comprehensive or exhaustive. They are supplied to show teachers useful examples. Teachers, or groups of teachers, might create one to three forms each year to fit specific assignments in their school or classroom.

(text continues on page 18)

Figure 2.1   Composition Evaluation

Note to teacher: This form allows teachers to indicate students' progress in areas that need improvement. It is especially helpful to beginning writers and provides guidance and encouragement. This form might be used in grade 4 or 5 for a paper that emphasized focus, details, and vivid language.*

Idea Focus

1	2	3	4	5
Try again. Think about what you're writing about. What is the main focus?		You're moving. Keep working.		Sounds great! I'm proud of you.

Details

1	2	3	4	5
Try again. Add more details.		You have some good details, but still more are needed.		Very descriptive. Lots of details

Describing and Action Words

1	2	3	4	5
Try again. Use words that paint a picture or show an action.		This is much better.		Good. Your word choices are excellent.

Punctuation and Capitalization

1	2	3	4	5
Many sentences do not begin with capitals. Many sentences do not have the correct punctuation. Show it to your group or partner again. See if you need more help.		Several errors. Proofread carefully.		Almost all sentences begin with capital letters and have correct punctuation.

Overall Impression

1	2	3	4	5
Keep trying.		It looks pretty good.		Beautiful!

*It never hurts to point out technical errors or overall impression.

Form 2.1   Some Examples of Integrated Elements and Assessment Tips for "Writers Are Readers and Thinkers, Too"

Lesson	Math	Science	Social Studies	Technology	Arts Plus: Art, Drama, Music, PE	Assessment Tips and Other Notes
Prewriting: Working With Perspective	x			x	x	After students develop a story or poem, assess based on vocabulary usage and punctuation; extend as needed.
Prewriting: Exploring Color		x	x	x	x	Group activity; assess using participation guidelines, Form 2.2.
Prewriting: Using Music		x		x	x	Group activity; use participation guidelines, Form 2.1; reward students for extending vocabulary.
Drafting: Choosing topics from any content area	x	x	x	x	x	Check work for basic factual information; assess students for following instructions.

Responding and Revising	X	X	X	X	X	Students check factual information; assess specific conventions as covered in class, such as punctuation, spelling, grammar, organization, and word usage.
Publishing	X	X	X	X	X	Use composition evaluation, Figure 2.1, or devise your own. See Writing Final Assessment in the Appendix.
All Lessons	X	X	X	X	X	Provide opportunities for self-assessment (Caitlyn Flowers; Writing Final Assessment; and the Critics' Choice, Appendix), permitting the teacher to assess what students have learned from specific lessons, leading to new explorations and ongoing refinement.

Form 2.2   Participation Grading Guidelines

Note to teacher: This evaluation based solely on participation is appropriate at times, especially when your students are working in an unfamiliar area. This form is shown and explained to students but is used by the teacher.

5   Student listens and participates in ways that show exceptional interest and understanding.

4   Student listens and participates in ways that show increased interest and understanding.

3   Student listens and participates in basically acceptable ways.

2   Student listens and participates minimally.

1   Student often does not listen or participate.

SUMMARY

The steps of the writing process are prewriting, drafting, responding and revising, proofreading and editing, publishing, and assessment. Implicit in this chapter is an emphasis on the four strands of language—listening, speaking, reading, and writing—and their relevance to critical thinking throughout this process. The steps of the writing process transform a concept (idea) into a product (finished composition).

RESOURCES

Arbuthnot, May Hill. (1964). *Children and Books.* Glenview, IL: Scott Foresman. Excellent resource for teachers and students of children's literature.

Bernstein, Elmer. (n.d.). Roll in the Tire. On *Music From the Motion Picture, To Kill a Mockingbird* [LP recording]. Hollywood, CA: Ava Records. The dramatic musical shift can be used to structure a written piece.

Bryan, Ashley. (1987). *Beat the Story Drum, Pum-Pum.* New York: Atheneum. Five Nigerian folktales illustrated with woodcuts and retold in rhythmic language.

Bryan, Ashley. (1999). *The Night Has Ears: African Proverbs.* New York: Atheneum. A beautifully illustrated book of proverbs, which students can use as patterns for writing their own.

Calkins, Lucy McCormick. (1983). *Lessons From a Child: On the Teaching and Learning of Writing.* London: Heinemann Educational Books.

Charlie Daniels Band. (1979). The Devil Went Down to Georgia. On *Million Mile Reflections* [LP recording]. New York: CBS/Epic Records. Several versions have been recorded by Daniels and others. Preview the lyrics.

dePaola, Tomie. (1978). *Pancakes for Breakfast.* New York: Harcourt Brace Javonovich. A picture book with limited text, which students can use for writing their own stories.

dePaola, Tomie. (1983). *Sing, Pierrot, Sing.* New York: Harcourt Brace Javonovich. A picture book without text, which students can use for writing their own stories.

Graves, Donald. (1983). *Writing: Teachers and Children at Work.* Exeter, NH: Heinemann. Writing is explored as central to literacy education.

Joplin, Scott. (1973). Pineapple Rag. On *The Sting* [LP record]. Universal City, CA: MCA Records. Music which illustrates unity of theme.

Lobel, Arnold. (1980). *Fables.* New York: Harper & Row. Modern fables that may be used as story patterns.

MacDonald, Suse, and Oakes, Bill. (1988). *Numblers.* New York: Dial Books for Young Readers. Shapes of numbers are manipulated to make pictures.

National Council of Teachers of English. Retrieved July 23, 2002, from www.ncte.org. This Web site has information and links to current research regarding all strands of language development.

National Reading Panel. (2000). Press Releases and Congressional Testimony. Retrieved July 23, 2002, from www. nationalreadingpanel.org/Press/press_releases.htm

National Writing Project. (2002, March). *Profiles of the National Writing Project.* Retrieved July 27, 2002, from www. writingproject.org/Publications/other/index.html

O'Neill, Mary. (1989). *Hailstones and Halibut Bones.* New York: Delacorte. A poetry book of colors personified.

Ragtimes and Cakewalks Played by Antique Musical Boxes. Camden, NJ: Recorded Publications. Recorded tunes from old-fashioned music boxes.

CHAPTER THREE

Mathematics in the Real World

Philosophy is written in this grand book—I mean the universe—which continually stands open to our gaze, but it cannot be understood unless one first learns to comprehend the language and interpret the characters in which it is written . . . mathematics. . . .

—Galileo Galilei (Bartlett's Familiar Quotations)

In 1989, the National Council of Teachers of Mathematics (NCTM) developed its *Curriculum and Evaluation Standards for School Mathematics,* in which they recommended a move away from traditional mathematics teaching, emphasizing routine skills development, and toward a curriculum which promotes higher-order thinking skills. Of late, more and more is being written stressing the importance of giving students hands-on, real-world situations in which to use mathematics. In addition, research suggests that students need to spend more time in math instruction and to cover subjects in more depth than in the past.

In *Edtalk, What We Know About Mathematics Teaching and Learning,* Nancy Kober builds on the NCTM standards as well as recent research and scholarship. She summarizes those things which must occur for students to succeed in math classes:

- *Student Attitudes.* Positive attitudes toward math help build good math students. Teachers' attitudes must reflect the idea that math is "challenging, fun, and useful." (p. 7)

- *Relevance.* To convince students that math is relevant, "use problems and examples from everyday life . . . ; develop class projects that connect math to the real world . . . ; bring in parents and community people to discuss how they use mathematics in their jobs." (p. 8)

- *Mathematics Content.* Research findings suggest that students do not receive enough math instruction. In elementary schools, in particular, "too much math content focuses on computational skills—including long-division and square roots that are seldom used in adult life—at the expense of higher order thinking skills, such as problem solving, conceptualization, applications, and reasoning." (p. 9)

- *Subject Integration.* Math and science are frequently paired, but this should be a starting point, not a limitation; "social studies, reading, writing, and even art, music, and physical education can be partnered with math." (p. 13)

- *Higher-Order Skills.* Students should be challenged "to search for patterns and connections; to create representations and explanations, to use a variety of strategies to work problems and check solutions; and to apply prior knowledge to new information." (p. 17)

- *Active Instruction.* This includes a variety of approaches, such as small-group, cooperative learning, hands-on experiences, and use of concrete objects or manipulatives, all of which will lead to higher-order thinking skills. (p. 19)

This summary suggests that successful math instruction requires a break from the traditional methods of teaching and the development of new strategies. With math, we often become bogged down in teaching computation or how to use a calculator and forget that these things make more sense given a real-world context where students can apply the knowledge they are gaining. In the remainder of this chapter, we provide examples of lessons which begin as math lessons but evolve and are integrated into other subject areas. In such a way, students begin by learning necessary math skills and continue to use those skills in real-world contexts, thus developing higher-order thinking skills and participating in relevant instruction. At the end of each lesson, we list the most applicable primary characteristics from Kober's list. Teachers can easily adapt our lessons to their circumstances or create additional lessons based on the following:

- *Student attitudes*—developing positive attitudes toward math
- *Relevance*—linking mathematics to the real world
- *Mathematics content*—teaching topics in depth
- *Subject integration*—using math in *all* subject areas
- *Higher-order skills*—making connections and representations, communicating, reasoning, and problem solving
- *Active instruction*—using a variety of approaches

TEACHING MATHEMATICS THROUGH MONEY

Learning the denominations of money and how to add, subtract, multiply, and divide amounts of money is an integral part of mathematics. The study of fractions and decimals also fits seamlessly into the study of money and thus becomes more relevant. Using money makes the instruction practical and opens up dozens of additional possibilities for mathematics lessons.

Example 1: Coins and Dollar Bills—Grades 1 and 2

As students become more proficient with counting, teaching them about denominations of money and how to count money is an important lesson. Once they have learned to count to 100, you can begin to have them count denominations. First-grade students can begin to add and subtract whole number amounts, and second-grade students can practice subtraction of monetary denominations to reinforce the skill of borrowing.

To begin, give students copies of as many denominations of play money as possible. Include pennies, nickels, dimes, quarters, 50-cent pieces, and dollar bills. Discuss how much each denomination is worth—a dime is 10 cents, a nickel is 5 cents, and so on. Also, discuss the different signs used when writing money amounts and their placement next to the amounts (the ¢ comes after the amount and the $ is placed before the amount: 25¢ or $1). Provide all students with their own set of play money and ask them to count each denomination and write down how many of each they have. It is a good idea to have one or two sets of real money available, so students understand how to differentiate between the various denominations, such as a penny and a dime, which are similar in size and appearance.

Some students might create the following addition problems from the play or real money given them:

Pennies	Nickels	Dimes	Quarters	Fifty
9	4	3	3	1
1	5	10	25	
1	5	10	25	+50
1	5	+10	+25	
1	+5			
1				
1				
1				
1				
+1				

After adding the amounts in the columns of their charts, second-grade students can write problems which involve addition and subtraction of amounts from different columns in the chart. For example:

$$\begin{array}{ccc} 50¢ & 75¢ & 50¢ \\ \underline{-9¢} & \underline{+30¢} & \underline{-20¢} \end{array}$$

Once students have developed their math problems, they can pass the problems to a classmate to complete. To extend these activities, set up a very modest class store. All items in the store will be class materials—no real sales will take place. Stock the store with such items as pencils, markers, erasers, and paper that can be "purchased" for prices arrived at by adding the play money denominations which students have been given previously (a pencil might be 15¢ and a marker 23¢). Begin the math lesson each day by allowing students to "go to the store." Allow students to buy items to use for the day by figuring out how many of each

---

Box 3.1   Primary Characteristics of Money Lessons, Grades 1 and 2

- **Mathematics Content.** Students not only learn about numbers and operations by practicing counting, adding, and subtracting but also extend their knowledge into monetary denominations where they are asked to reason in order to develop problems using the play money they have been given.

- **Relevance.** Using money immediately makes this a real-world lesson, which is further extended by the addition of a class store in which students communicate regarding the money they have and the item they wish to purchase, problem solve regarding the cost of items, and make connections about amounts of money and purchasing ability.

---

kind of coin will be required to purchase the particular item. Students who can successfully add the correct amounts can purchase the desired items. Encourage students to work in groups of three or four to figure out difficult addition problems so everyone can succeed. Box 3.1 gives an overview of money lessons for Grades 1 and 2.

Learning about money continues to be important as students move from grade to grade. Fourth- and fifth-grade students can use money problems to practice division skills, and fifth- and sixth-grade students can use money to learn about fractions and decimals. Using money problems as a basis for learning these skills makes it easy to integrate math into other subject areas. The following examples delineate ways that such integration can occur.

Example 2: Planning a Trip—Grades 4, 5, and 6

An exciting way to involve students in the study of math is by incorporating travel with the study of different regions of the United States or of the world. Students use their knowledge of

Table 3.1   Sample Spreadsheet

Expenses	Day 1	Day 2	Day 3	Day 4	Day 5	Totals
Hotel	$65.95	$88.98	$75.45	$55.40	$155.65	$441.43
Meals	$37.95	$28.85	$44.19	$33.20	$75.50	$219.69
Transportation	$28.99	$28.99	$28.99	$28.99	$28.99	$144.95
Activities	$15.10	$25.15	$35.50	$25.65	$25.95	$127.35
Souvenirs	$10.50	$12.50	$50.00	$35.00	$55.00	$163.00
Gifts	$0.00	$0.00	$15.00	$65.00	$10.00	$90.00
Totals	$158.49	$184.47	$249.13	$243.24	$351.09	
Grand Total						**$1,186.42**

money by planning their spending for such a trip. Travel guides give approximate costs that can be encountered in various cities and allow students to estimate how much they will spend and how much money will be needed for the trip. You can collect menus from restaurants or advertisements from the newspaper to demonstrate costs for meals; the travel section of most big-city newspapers provides costs of hotels, motels, car rental, and tourist activities that might be involved. Students or teachers can also do Internet research for information about costs. After students produce lists of items which they believe they may spend money on, give them mock checkbooks or have them develop spreadsheets on the computer (see Table 3.1).

To integrate more mathematical concepts, have students use maps to plot their travel routes and develop graphs and charts to record travel speed, travel time, and distance as well as predicted arrival times. The goal might be for students to stay within the budgets they have set for themselves, yet arrive home from the trip with souvenirs for the family.

Additionally, students can learn about different modes of travel and allot time for activities based on travel times and other pertinent information (see Box 3.2). Showing videos of different cities, states, and countries helps students become more involved in the make-believe trip.

Example 3: School Store—Grades 5 and 6

Students learn about the value of money and the importance of correct record keeping in setting up a real school store. This

---

**Box 3.2   Primary Characteristics
of Planning a Trip**

- **Relevance.** Students are asked to use their math skills to plan activities that are actually possible. They immediately see the uses of the math they are learning.

- **Subject Integration.** Students use math skills while conducting social studies activities, thus learning that subject areas often integrate with each other.

- **Student Attitudes.** Using math in the real-world situation of planning a trip and incorporating information about areas around the world provides students with views into different cities, states, and countries. As they integrate math into a variety of activities, their interest and excitement grows tremendously, and the usefulness of mathematics study is no longer in question.

---

provides them with lots of practice in addition, subtraction, multiplication, and division facts and skills while avoiding spending too much time in drill and practice situations.

The store should contain only such items as pens, pencils, and notebook paper that students will need during the course of the school day. Assign different jobs to different students and rotate the jobs weekly. Help students define workable hours of operation of the store—before and after school, during recess, and so on. Using a computer if it's available, set up a spreadsheet for a ledger to keep a record of what was purchased, by whom, and how much they paid. Determine prices of items and how modest profits will be used. Students should be responsible for counting money both at the beginning and at the end of the day, for keeping track of inventory, and for making correct change when purchases are made. Students practice calculation skills before the store opens to see if the change they give and receive is correct and then double-check themselves by using a calculator to complete the spreadsheet or ledger page. See Box 3.3 for a summary of the advantages of a school store.

Box 3.3   Primary Characteristics of a School Store, Grades 5 and 6

- **Mathematics Content.** Setting up a store is an ongoing project in which students are constantly asked to use their math skills for new and different applications.

- **Higher-Order Thinking Skills.** Students are asked to make connections between mathematics skills and problems to be solved as well as to use reasoning skills in a variety of situations provided by the store.

- **Active Instruction.** The school store provides hands-on opportunities for students to use their math skills in very concrete ways while maintaining an atmosphere of fun and excitement.

TEACHING MATHEMATICS THROUGH MEASUREMENT

Like money, the concept of measurement provides study throughout elementary school. Students learn about standard measurement, methods of measuring, and conversion from one type of measurement to another.

Example 1: Measuring Familiar Objects—Grades K-2

Beginning in kindergarten, students should be introduced to the concept of measurement. In the early grades, it is crucial to make all the lessons as real and familiar as possible.

Bring cartons and containers of varying sizes—half-pint, pint, quart, half-gallon, and gallon and use circle time to discuss things that students notice about these containers. Demonstrate for students that each contains exactly one-half the volume of the next bigger size by pouring colored liquid from one container to the next starting with the smallest, or pour from the gallon to all the rest of the sizes and ask students to guess, or estimate, how much they think is left in the gallon container. As a follow-up, you may also want to show students different sizes of measuring cups and spoons and take time with them to examine these measuring devices.

In the first and second grades, students can add information about linear measurement to their body of knowledge. An interesting way to open a discussion of linear measurement is to discuss measurement and the need for a standard. Provide students with linear measuring devices in different lengths, such as 6- and 12-inch rulers and yardsticks, and have students examine them closely. Ask students why they think the 12-inch ruler is also called a foot. Explain to students that the original measurement was based on the length of the human foot, and then have them take off their shoes and measure the actual length of their own feet. Once students have done this and written down the exact measurement, they should compare their measurements to those of their classmates.

Now ask students to measure the width of their desks and help them figure out how many feet the desks are across if they use their own foot length. Students will easily realize that if everyone has a different idea regarding the length of a foot, then no measurement can ever be accepted as standard. (Students who are familiar with horses may also realize that the height of a horse is measured in hands, now standardized as four inches but, like the foot, originally based on the human body part.)

Once students are familiar with the concept of measurement, have them examine rulers and yardsticks for comparison. They should realize that there are 12 inches in a foot and 3 feet in a yard. Also point out to them that the inches are divided into smaller parts or fractions, such as half and quarter inches, and discuss the concept of fractions. When students are familiar with the various measurements, divide them into groups and have them measure different items within the classroom, such as the teacher's desk, one wall, the width of a window or door, the tiles on the floor, or an unsharpened pencil. One student should do the measuring and give the information to another student who keeps the figures. A third student can then add the lengths for various items until they have accurate total measurements. A fourth student presents the findings of the group to the class. Students can be assessed on the accuracy of their measurements, their

---

Box 3.4   Primary Characteristics of Measuring Familiar Objects Lesson, Grades K-2

- **Mathematics Content.** Students learn about different types of measurement as well as different measuring devices. They also look at standard measurement and why there is a need for such standards.

- **Higher-Order Thinking Skills.** Students are asked to make connections (for instance, between standards of measurement and their origins), communicate, and problem solve in order to understand types of measurement.

- **Student Attitudes.** Students learn that mathematics can be fun and challenging as well as useful. They see the usefulness of mathematics when they realize they can apply it to familiar situations.

---

addition, and their ability to work together. See Box 3.4 for a summary of the benefits of measuring familiar objects.

Example 2: Mealy Worms—Grades 3 and 4

As students move into upper elementary grades, they continue their study of measurement and also begin to learn about different systems of measurement. Students should begin to make connections between U.S. and metric systems of measurement and should practice converting measures from one system to the other.

Ms. Marni Hettena, fourth-grade teacher at The Fay School in Houston, Texas, has a fascinating project which enhances student math skills while integrating scientific material; this project involves mealy worms. Mealy worms can be purchased from pet stores selling fish and fish supplies or through science catalogs; they are easy to handle, not messy, require very little upkeep, and can be donated to a research lab at the end of the lesson.

After studying the life cycle of mealy worms, all students are given their own worm to raise. Students keep journals about the

---

Box 3.5   Primary Characteristics of Mealy Worm Measurement, Grades 3 and 4

- **Subject Integration.** Students learn very quickly that math plays an important role in science study. Math study becomes more relevant as it is tied to other areas.

- **Student Attitudes.** Students see that learning can be entertaining and that mathematics skills are used in a variety of settings. Students develop new perspectives on the uses of math skills.

- **Active Instruction.** Working with living creatures is very engaging for young students. Additionally, setting up races changes the dynamics of the classroom, allowing students to put math skills to use in unusual ways.

---

changes in their worms; they then measure worms daily and predict how soon the worms will turn into beetles. Students use graphs to keep track of this information. They also make comparisons between the worms' length in U.S. versus metric measurement. Students learn about data analysis and probability when they set up races between the worms in small arenas made of place mats.

They measure the track, time the events, and guess who will win based on data collected from other races. Box 3.5 gives characteristics of mealy worm measurement.

Figure 3.1 (page 31) uses decimals and inches for the measurements of the mealy worms, but fractions and centimeters can also be used in this project. You may wish to have students graph the information using both kinds of measurements. You may also wish to have students make bar graphs instead of, or in addition to, line graphs.

Example 3: The Alamo—Grades 4, 5, and 6

Ms. Hettena sees math possibilities in all subject areas. Another of her lessons stems from the study of Texas history.

Figure 3.1   Graph of Mealy Worm Growth

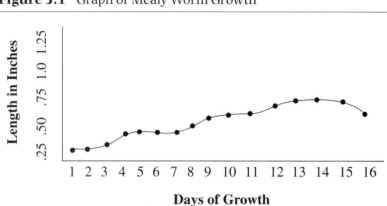

Ms. Hettena uses the Battle of the Alamo to help students develop real-world geometry skills, along with communication and representation skills (see Box 3.6). As students study the Battle of the Alamo, they learn that the actual mission building is not very large but played an enormous part in Texas history. Using their math skills of finding area, perimeter, length, width, height, pitch, and other geometric applications, students work in teams of about five students to build scale models of the Alamo. To do this, students must convert yards to centimeters and then determine what types of materials they can work with to build their models. Not only is Texas history brought to life, but students become immersed in real-world applications of the math they are learning. This is an easy lesson that can be used with any historical building in any state. A technology tie-in is to have students use the Internet to find Web sites which provide information about their state capitol building, such as dimensions and other pertinent architectural data.

OTHER SUGGESTED
MATH LESSONS FOR K-6

Example 1: "Numblers" for Any Grade

Math instruction need not always be the actual focal point of a lesson; art or writing or even physical education (PE) can help non-math and math students alike become more excited about the

---

Box 3.6   Primary Characteristics of the Alamo Project, Grades 4, 5, and 6

- **Higher-Order Thinking Skills.** Students are asked to make connections between systems of measurement, to represent information in the form of models, to problem solve ways to accomplish assignments, and to communicate about their work and their findings.

- **Subject Integration.** Students easily see that mathematics is used in several areas of study including history and science.

- **Relevance.** Students use measurement for purposes they may encounter as adult scientists, architects, builders, or even handy homeowners. They certainly experience how professionals use measurement.

---

possibilities of math as an interesting subject. An excellent example of how to begin such an approach can be seen using the book *Numblers* (MacDonald & Oakes), which we mentioned in Chapter 2. *Numblers* is an unusual counting book which presents the numerals 1 to 10 as they traditionally appear and then through a series of drawings transforms the numbers into other recognizable objects. For example, the numeral 1 becomes a seal standing up on its flippers. The illustrations in the book are fabulous and attract the attention of even the least interested math students at any elementary age.

Before introducing the book to students, you may wish to coordinate with the PE teacher to see about having the students construct exercises in which they use their bodies to form the numerals 1 to 10. If there is someone in your school who knows American Sign Language (ASL), you may also want to invite that person to demonstrate the signs or symbols for the numerals. By presenting students with these actual physical representations of symbolic characters, you can easily move into a demonstration of other transformations using the pictures in the book.

Once students have seen and discussed all the book illustrations, give them each a piece of unlined 11- by-17-inch paper and instruct them to choose any number from 1 to 100. Have them write that number in the middle of the sheet of paper as large as they would like. You will find that some students write tiny little numbers barely visible, and others write gigantic numbers which take up almost the whole page. Ask students to look at the numbers they have written, then to turn the page so that the number is on its side, then on its head, and then on its back. They should continue to look at the number from all different angles until they begin to see some shape in it other than the number. At this point, instruct them to flesh out the drawing with as many details as they choose.

As they draw, students should begin to jot down, on the back or in an upper corner, any words that come to mind as they work. When the drawings are finished, have students use these word banks to create stories about their drawings. Often, older elementary students will incorporate all kinds of mathematical information into their stories. At the end of the lesson, which may actually take 4 or 5 days to complete (working for an hour each day), have students share their drawings, pointing out the original numerals they started with, and then read their stories to their classmates. A further extension is to have students use word-processing software and type their stories, which can then be proofread and revised for a final edition to go with their artwork. The examples shown in Figures 3.2 and 3.3 demonstrate the different perspectives that students develop during an activity using *Numblers* and also show that this activity may be used with students of differing ages and ability or language levels.

Here is what Mamie wrote to go with her drawing (Figure 3.3):

House of Fives

By Mamie

There once lived a woman who lived in a house of fives. She had five children, five dresses, five pairs of shoes, and five plates on the table plus one more. She cooked five cakes, five pies, five small hams, five small turkeys, and five pieces of bread plus one. The food lasted for five days plus one more day. That's my story about the woman who lived in a house made of fives.

And here is an example of student writing by sixth grader Candezz Bell, Grissom Elementary School, writing on the use of the numeral 10:

(text continues on page 36)

Figure 3.2 First-Grade Student Example, Germiah May, MacArthur Elementary School, Houston, Texas: Use of the Numeral 7

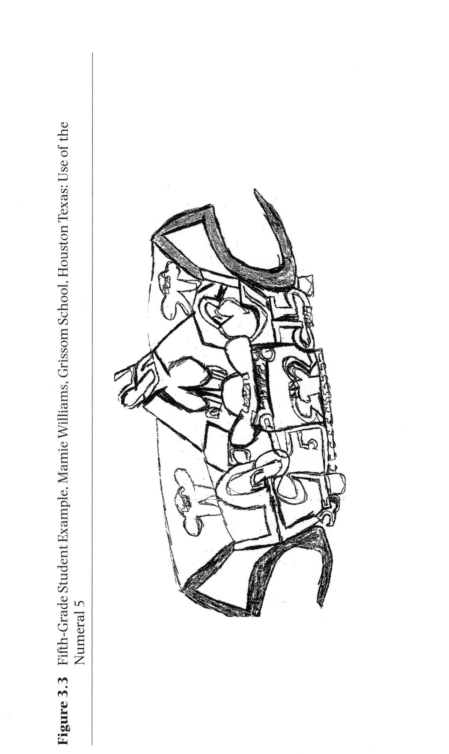

Figure 3.3 Fifth-Grade Student Example, Mamie Williams, Grissom School, Houston Texas: Use of the Numeral 5

> ### Box 3.7   Primary Characteristics of "Numblers" for Any Grade
>
> - **Higher-Order Thinking Skills.** Students learn to make connections between numbers and other shapes, to communicate about what they are doing, and to represent their ideas in unique ways. They also begin to develop a new perspective about the world around them.
>
> - **Subject Integration.** Students begin to look at mathematics differently, seeing the subject from many perspectives. The shapes of numerals themselves become prompts for writing and increased vocabulary study.

There once was a ride at Astroworld. It was called Ten. It was the shape of the number ten, and it fit ten people. Ten men made it. It was 10×10 feet high. It made a tour of Astroworld, which was ten acres wide. When you looked down, you saw ten sections of rides. You could see ten people walking in a group. There were ten trees in all at Astroworld. It took ten minutes to take a tour. I came ten times a month and got on the ride ten times. I stayed for ten hours. Over $5 + 5$ hundred people loved it. That's my ride Ten.

Once students have begun to look at mathematics differently, it will become easier and easier for you, the teacher, to integrate math into all kinds of lessons. Box 3.7 shows characteristics of "Numblers."

Example 2: Cooking Makes Math Delicious—Grades K and 1

One way to incorporate measurement into the classroom is through cooking. Use the book *The Gingerbread Man* (this classic comes in various editions), which many students study in kindergarten or first grade, as a starting point. After having the book read to them, students can make gingerbread cookies in class or the school kitchen, again learning about the real-world uses of measurement.

**Box 3.8   Primary Characteristics of
             Cooking Makes Math Delicious,
             for K-1**

- **Relevance.** Students easily make the connections between measurement and measuring when cooking. Measuring devices become much more meaningful when used to actually prepare food.

- **Subject Integration.** The study of food and cooking easily leads to further study in both social studies and science as well as reading.

Set up all the different measuring devices you will need. Lead students in a discussion of the different sizes of measuring cups and spoons. You can even introduce the concept of fractions by showing students that four 1/4-cup containers are equal to one cup, or that three teaspoons equal one tablespoon. Time can also be a part of the discussion as you talk about how long the cookies will take to bake and demonstrate the movement of the hands on the clock to the correct time.

An additional activity is to bake a large Gingerbread Man who "runs away." Involve the PE teacher in setting up physical activities where students "run, run as fast as you can" in some safe area of the school such as the gym while looking for the Gingerbread Man. Box 3.8 gives connections between cooking and math.

Example 3: Cooking Makes
Math Delicious—Grades 2, 3, and 4

Use cooking as a method to teach these students about weights and measures including fractions. One way to tie this to other subject areas is through the study of different cultures, which may be a part of any social studies class. Students can cook foods representative of various cultures, such as tacos where two tablespoons of cooked ground meat, one tablespoon of grated cheese, one-quarter cup of lettuce, and one teaspoon of salsa are added to a taco shell. In the process of creating a taco, students put their math skills to real use. The bonus is that students get to eat the tacos!

(text continues on page 42)

Form 3.1 Some Examples of Integrated Elements and Assessment Tips for "Mathematics in the Real World"

Lesson	Language Arts	Science	Social Studies	Technology	Arts Plus: Art, Drama, Music, PE	Assessment Tips and Other Notes
Planning a Trip	X	X	X			Use participation grading guidelines (Form 2.2). Base assessment on how well students do in reaching the goal of staying within the budget; grade students for correct use of mathematics in figuring costs and so on.
School Store	X	X	X			This is a collaborative activity; reward students for working well together and for problem solving. Give grades for record keeping and for correct mathematical work based on standards established at the beginning.

K-2 Measurement	X	X	X		Use participation grading guidelines (Form 2.2). Give grades based on accuracy of measurements taken and outcomes.
Mealy Worms	X	X			Assess the quality of journal entries based on prescribed requirements given to students at the beginning of the project. Assess the quality and the information provided in the chart; grade students' achievements in use of both U.S. and metric measurements.

(Continued)

Form 3.1 Continued

Lesson	Language Arts	Science	Social Studies	Technology	Arts Plus: Art, Drama, Music, PE	Assessment Tips and Other Notes
Alamo	X	X	X	X		Use participation grading guidelines (Form 2.2). Assess models based on requirements given at the beginning of the project. Grade students' scaling to produce the model.
Numblers	X			X	X	Use composition evaluation sheet (Figure 2.1). Grade final product on preset requirements such as use of capitals, punctuation, and vocabulary use.

Cooking Makes Math Delicious, K & 1	X	X	X		X	Use participation grading guidelines (Form 2.2). Assess students' understanding of measurement and telling time individually after the lessons are complete.
Cooking Makes Math Delicious, Grades 2, 3, and 4	X	X	X			Assess information presented about cultures based on requirements given at the beginning of the assignment. Use the Critics' Choice examples (see The Critics' Choice in the Appendix) or a writing final to have students assess what they have learned.

To integrate science with all the other subjects covered by a cooking lesson, lead students in a discussion of the physical properties of the dry ingredients and how adding liquid or heat or leavening changes those properties.

When all the cooking is complete, have students write stories about visiting foreign lands and enjoying the foods of those lands. Incorporate geography into the lesson by discussing why certain types of foods are eaten in certain parts of the world—for example, the terrain and growing conditions which make some plants easy to grow and others impossible. See Form 3.1 (pages 38-41) for examples of integrated elements and assessment for the various lessons in this chapter.

SUMMARY

Students at all elementary grades need to spend more time studying math but not only basic facts and computation. Students need to be involved in real-world uses of math and to develop the higher-order thinking skills which those uses require. Integrating math with other subject areas makes it much easier for teachers to break away from drill and practice sheets as math becomes exciting, useful, and interesting to all students.

RESOURCES

Adler, David. (1995). *Calculator Riddles.* New York: Holiday House. Riddles to be solved using a calculator; Grades 3 to 6.

Axelrod, Amy. (1994). *Pigs Will Be Pigs: Fun With Math and Money.* New York: Simon & Schuster. A pig family with an empty fridge and $1 has to add, subtract, multiply, and divide to get enough to eat; Grades K-6.

Aylesworth, Jim. (1998). *The Gingerbread Man.* New York: Scholastic. An old tale retold.

Braddon, Kathryn, Hall, Nancy J., & Taylor, Dale. (1993). *Math Through Children's Literature.* Englewood, CO: Teacher Ideas Press. Provides summaries of children's books related to NCTM standards.

Carle, Eric. (1987). *The Very Hungry Caterpillar.* New York: Philomel. A counting book which covers days of the weeks and food varieties; Grades K-2.

Davies, Glyn. (2002). *A History of Money From Ancient Times to the Present Day*. Cardiff: University of Wales Press. An extensive amount of information for teachers on money and its uses throughout history.

Hopkins, Lee Bennett (Ed.). (1997). *Marvelous Math: A Book of Poems*. New York: Simon & Schuster. A collection of poems on math subjects; Grades 3 to 6.

Hurst, Carol Otis, & Otis, Rebecca. (1996). *Picturing Math*. New York: SRA/McGraw-Hill. An annotated list of picture books with ideas for integration with math content.

Kober, Nancy. (1996). *Edtalk, What We Know About Mathematics Teaching and Learning*. Washington, DC: Council for Educational Development and Research.

MacDonald, Suse, & Oakes, Bill. (1988). *Numblers*. New York: Dial Books for Young Readers.

National Council of Teachers of Mathematics. (2000). *Curriculum and Evaluation Standards for School Mathematics*. Reston, VA: Author. Retrieved July 27, 2002, from www.nctm.org

Patilla, Peter. (1998). *Fun With Numbers*. Brookfield, CT: Millbrook Press. A book of picture puzzles to identify the numbers 1 to 10; Grades 2 to 5.

Schwartz, David M., & Kellogg, Steven. (1985). *How Much Is a Million?* New York: Scholastic. Text and pictures to help students conceptualize numerals such as million, billion, trillion; Grades K-3.

Van Cleave, Janice. (1998). *Janice Van Cleave's Play and Find Out About Math: Easy Activities for Young Children*. New York: J. Wiley. Step-by-step instructions for 50 simple math activities and experiments; Grades K-3.

CHAPTER FOUR

Science Is Sensory

Man can learn nothing unless he proceeds from the known to the unknown.

—Claude Bernard (Bartlett's Familiar Quotations)

One of the most difficult things for a teacher to do is to teach everything that is supposed to be taught during the course of a day or a week. For younger students, the obvious emphasis must be on language arts and mathematics, because these subject areas provide the foundation for all other subject areas. However, in the push to teach these two subject areas well, science in particular often gets pushed into the background and only addressed when extra time can be found. Consequently, students advance to junior high or middle school ill equipped to deal with science courses, which now occupy a strong place in the curriculum. Some students who were consistently at the top of their classes suddenly find themselves struggling to keep up in science.

The question is, How do we emphasize language arts and mathematics without cheating science? As we said in Chapter 2, writing crosses all boundaries: It is part of science, social studies, math, and every other subject. The same can be said of reading—no subject can be thoroughly studied without an ability to read. So the answer should be apparent: Integrate the study of science with the study of language arts and particularly with reading and writing.

THE SCIENTIFIC PROCESS

To begin with, even in kindergarten, it is important to emphasize scientific thinking and the process which needs to be followed for scientific study. This scientific method requires the following steps:

Step I: Make observations.

Step II: Form a hypothesis.

Step III: Gather data.

Step IV: Analyze the data.

Step V: Draw conclusions.

Even the youngest children can observe an animal or flower or rock, make some guesses about the observation, and go on to engage in the scientific method.

Most teachers are aware of this method of teaching science but are not always able to incorporate it into the classroom. Some ideas follow which encourage scientific learning.

Step I: Make Observations

To make observations, students must first have something to observe. This means using the entire classroom as a science lab. Students often learn scientific information best when they can approach it in a sensory manner; they need to touch, smell, see, hear, and taste (sometimes). To enhance scientific learning, provide interesting items for children to observe.

• Create earth science observation centers in the classroom and stock them, for instance, with whatever rocks and minerals can be found—parents who are geologists or even amateur rockhounds will often gladly donate to such a cause.

• Have students bring in samples of rocks, shells, and minerals they have found on family trips, on walks around the family farm, or in the neighborhood to contribute to your observation center. Use

Form 4.1   Observation Chart, Grade 3

Item	Descriptors			
	Texture	Color	Weight	Other
Large rock from playground	Smooth	Gray and black	Very heavy	Does not chip
Conch shell	Rough outside, smooth inside	White outside, pink inside	Heavy	Can hear sound when held to ear
Sandstone from New Mexico	Very rough and crumbly	Brown, tan, red	Very light	Breaks into sand easily
Small, rounded shell	Grooved, sort of smooth	Gray and black outside, white inside	Light	No sound

new contributions to develop discussions about creatures who live in shells; or types of rocks; or to start a discussion of wind, water, and soil erosion; or about any other appropriate subject.

• Read aloud or have students read stories, poems, plays, and chapters from their science books. As a part of the discussion, pass around the objects from the observation center. Have students compare the way the objects look with the descriptions in the materials they read. Students can then write their own descriptions and compare and contrast their descriptions with those in the reading.

• Using a chart similar to Form 4.1, have students make observations about the items in the earth science observation center. Begin as a whole class discussion, then allow students to observe items in small groups or individually. Providing a column such as "Other" allows students to make note of things which interest them and of which some may not be aware.

• Start a "marine life center" by bringing in an old aquarium, or even a large fishbowl, and purchasing a couple of goldfish; or by asking someone at a pet store to donate them. Allow children to observe the cycle of life as it is played out in this minipond. Assign different students to feed and clean the aquarium, and use cleaning as an opportunity to discuss possible occurrences which may result from underfeeding, overfeeding, undercleaning, overcleaning, the introduction of too much chlorinated water, or allowing too much or too little sunlight into the tank. In rural areas, students often find tadpoles and other creatures which can easily become part of this center and provide hours of observation.

• Go to the seafood market, if possible, and buy a whole fish (such as a snapper or bass), a live crawfish, and a squid. Read or have students read stories such as *Fish Is Fish* by Leo Lionni, a wonderful picture book about a tadpole and a minnow who grow up together and then discover their differences. Allow students to hold and examine the whole fish you have purchased and look at its gills.

• Compare this to a frog which begins life in water but then is able to breathe oxygen from the air and so is able to travel away from the water. Compare the scales of the fish to the slippery, bumpy skin of the frog. Now look at the crawfish and squid. Discuss the different ways that these creatures move through water and on land. Make charts for delineating the similarities and differences. Follow up by having students write and illustrate their own short stories about the creatures they have observed. The chart in Form 4.2 provides an easy way for students to look for specific similarities and differences among the items being observed. It aids students in their observation and helps to keep them on the task at hand—the particular kinds of observations you want them to be making.

• For an animal life center, get a small carrying cage and house some gerbils or hamsters in it. After the children have

Form 4.2   Marine Life Chart, Grade 3

Questions	Type of Creature			
	Snapper	**Frog**	**Crawfish**	**Squid**
How does it breathe?				
What kind of skin does it have?				
How does it move in water?				
How does it move on land?				

learned about care and feeding of the animals, allow a different child to take the creatures home and care for them each weekend during the year. In class, read stories about different animals; allow the students to touch the class pets and to observe the way they move. Students should notice the twitching of their noses and the way that they scurry around. Students also should be aware of eating and sleeping habits. Have students write and illustrate reports, short stories, and poems about the animals.

• Demonstrate plant life by allowing children to plant bean seeds in small plastic cups filled with potting soil. Clear plastic cups will allow students to actually observe the roots growing on the plants. Punch holes in the bottoms of the cups to provide drainage. Place some cups in full sunlight and others in partial shade. Remind students to water their plants regularly and then use every opportunity to observe the effects of too much or too little sun and water. If you have room and approval, plant a garden and allow students to plant real crops of flowers and vegetables which grow well in your area. Ask an interested parent with knowledge of gardening to come in and help students plan their garden. These gardens can actually be planted in very small areas, as long as there is plenty of light and water is accessible.

Students should be responsible for proper planting techniques, and classes should read and discuss the planting methods as described on seed packages. Students may want to track weather changes to know when to water and when plants may need to be protected from the elements. This is also an excellent way to open a discussion on types of soil and plant growing habits and needs. Have students keep journals of all the activities required to grow a garden—planning the size of the bed, checking available sunlight for the area before beginning to dig, adding soil and fertilizer, actually planting the seeds or plants, watching the growing process, checking water and soil amendments required, and finally enjoying the flower and fruit or vegetable production. The journal page in Figure 4.1 is from a special summer gardening project conducted by the mother of a student.

- During recess, take the students outside to lie in the grass or sit on the sidewalk and observe cloud formations, how the wind affects the plants, and what happens to the soil when there isn't enough rain. If your school has access to magnifying glasses or a telescope, use them for better observation of anything from clouds to insects.

- At snack time or when a selection from the reading curriculum allows for it, offer students different foods such as apples and oranges, crackers, and cookies; discuss the different tastes of each food. Introduce the concepts of *sweet, sour,* and *salty* tastes and *crisp, mushy,* and *soft* textures.

Step II: Form a Hypothesis

Now that the students have something to observe and have made some notes or lists, they can begin to form hypotheses based

Figure 4.1   Journal Page Example, Victoria Arceneaux, Grade 5

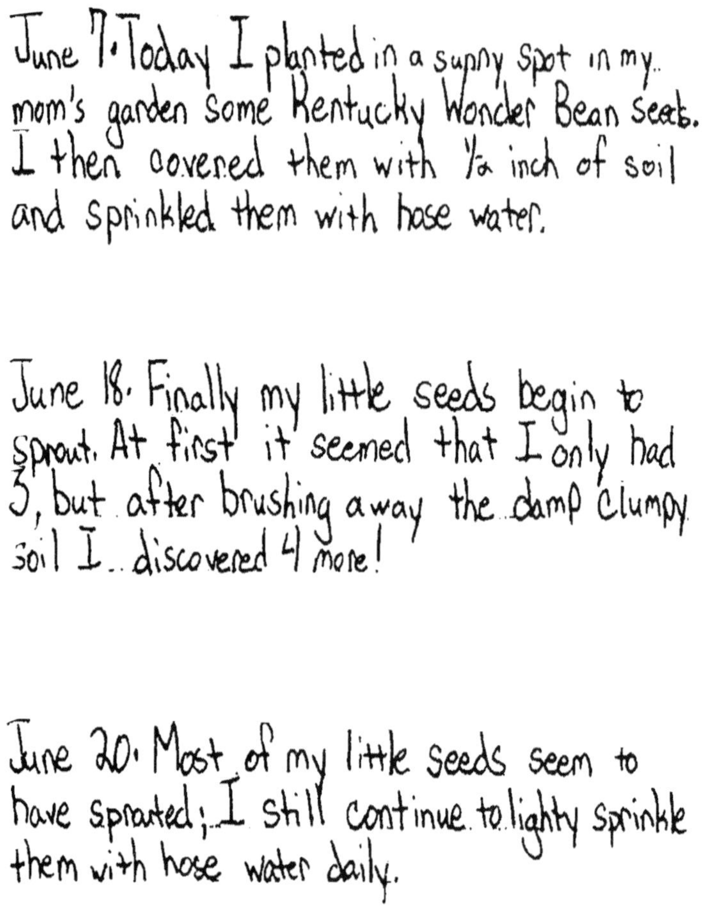

June 7. Today I planted in a sunny spot in my mom's garden some Kentucky Wonder Bean seeds. I then covered them with 1/2 inch of soil and sprinkled them with hose water.

June 18. Finally my little seeds begin to sprout. At first it seemed that I only had 3, but after brushing away the damp clumpy soil I discovered 4 more!

June 20. Most of my little seeds seem to have sprouted; I still continue to lightly sprinkle them with hose water daily.

on their observations. A simple example of forming a hypothesis can be done as part of a taste test in kindergarten or first grade. Purchase at least four different varieties and colors of apples at the grocery store. Wash and slice most of the apples (reserve one whole apple of each variety for students to observe size) and place them on individual paper plates—one plate per variety. Pass around slices of the different varieties for students to see, touch, and smell. Depending on the age-group, make a chart on the board or have students make their own charts on which to record information. Ask students to record information regarding differences in smell, feel, and color (see Form 4.3—this type of form simply helps students make a hypothesis). Once this information has been recorded, ask students to form an opinion about which variety of apples will be sweet and which will be sour; which will be crisp and which will be mushy.

Younger students may need examples of other things which are sweet and sour to taste first, such as sweet candy and sour balls, to fully understand the concept of sweet and sour. Have students write down or dictate their hypotheses and what they are based on—for example, "I think the Granny Smith apple will be crisp because when I pushed on it with my finger, it did not crush. The Rome apple felt squishy in my hand, so I think it will taste mushy. The Gala apple is green, so I think it will be sour, but the Red Delicious looks like it will be sweet. The Fuji had no strong smell, and it is red and yellow, so I am not sure what it will taste like."

Step III: Gather Data

Since the actual hypothesis can only be tested by having students taste the apple, that is the next step in gathering data. Pass each student a piece of each type of apple and a couple of saltine crackers. Explain that students need to taste one type of apple and record their observations, then taste a bite of the cracker to "clean their palates" for more accurate tastes of the other apple varieties. Have the students taste each type of apple with a bite of cracker in between and then record their observations in a format such as Form 4.4 (page 53).

Step IV: Analyze the Data

After the students have completed their taste tests and recorded their conclusions, hold a class discussion in which students reveal their hypotheses and then the data that they recorded after each taste. Discuss the kind of information that students used to form

Form 4.3   Hypothesis Worksheet, Grade 2

Fill in your hypotheses about taste and texture of the apples we have observed in class.

Hypothesis Example: I think the _yellow delicious_ will be _mushy_ because _it is yellow_.

Hypothesis I: I think the _____ will be _____

because _____

Hypothesis II: I think the _____ will be _____

because _____

their hypotheses and which information proved to be useful or accurate and which didn't. For instance, in Form 4.4, students used color, size, feel, and smell to predict taste and texture, but the data show that size and color are not good predictors of these features.

Step V: Draw Conclusions

Once all students have had a chance to talk about their observations, ask them to record their conclusions about the apples. Which did they find to be sweet or sour, crisp or mushy? Did their finding match their original predictions? Can certain traits such as color and hardness help in choosing apples to eat? Is there any other information which may help in the selection of apples for different uses such as pies, caramel apples, apple sauce, and so forth?

Ask students to look at their data charts and draw conclusions by completing the information about the six observed features in a conclusions chart such as Form 4.5 (page 54).

After conducting the experiment above, students should have a clear concept of the scientific method. And with all the centers set up in the classroom, they now have plenty of things to observe for future lessons. Following are three additional lessons that can follow the same steps with the same emphasis on writing, reading, and scientific method.

Form 4.4   Data Table, Grades K-2

Data Obs.	Gala	Gr. Smith	R. Del.	Y. Del.	Rome	Fuji	Jonathan
Color	Red and green	Bright green	Dark red	Yellow	Red	Pale red	Dark red
Size & Shape	Medium round	Large round	Large oval	Large oval	Medium round	Small round	Small round
Feel	Medium hard	Hard	Medium soft	Soft	Very soft	Hard	Hard
Smell	Sweet	Sweet & sour	Very sweet	None	None	Sort of sweet	Sour & sweet
Taste	Mildly sweet	Sour	Bland	No taste	Slightly sweet	Slightly sweet	Sour
Texture	Crisp	Very crisp	Mushy	Mushy	Mushy	Sort of crisp	Slightly crisp

Form 4.5   Conclusions, Grades 3-6

> Your experiment is about the taste and texture of apples. Based on what you have learned from the data, what do you conclude about the importance of
>
> **Color**
>
> **Size**
>
> **Shape**
>
> **Smell**
>
> regarding the taste and texture of apples ?

APPLICATIONS AT VARIOUS GRADE LEVELS

Example 1: Kindergartners in the Meadow

In Deborah Rommel's kindergarten class at The Fay School in Houston, Texas, students combine literature and science with reading, writing, and technology. Students read counting books, such as Paul Galdone's *Over in the Meadow*, and then participate in a variety of activities drawn from the book's content.

To observe, they talk about all the things found in the meadow according to the book; students draw pictures of three or four items that may be found in a meadow. Students then form hypotheses about what may be living in the "meadow" (any area around the school which may have grass, flowers, and creatures such as lizards and ladybugs to observe). They walk outside to gather data and investigate green grass and bluebonnets or other wildflowers growing in the "meadow" around the school. They search for lizards, bugs, and wildlife such as frogs or toads. Returning to the classroom, students analyze the data and discuss the animals that live in the meadow and what type of environment is required for each animal. Some of these animals such as frogs, lizards, and even mice, are housed in classroom centers on a semipermanent basis, but students may bring in others for show-and-tell.

In computer class they produce books on the various aspects of the meadow—students draw pictures of creatures, grass, flowers, ponds, and others things from the meadow and then dictate to teachers, who type the stories to go with the pictures (see Figure 4.2, page 56).

At circle time, students present drawings and handwritten books on the subject; in general, every activity is derived from the meadow. Finally students draw conclusions about where certain types of creatures live and what types of plant life can be found in the area of the school and around their homes.

Example 2: Sea Life in Second Grade

Students in second grade at The Fay School learn reading, writing, and public speaking as skills fully integrated with science. For instance, in a unit on sea life, the teacher, Jan Doherty, introduces the unit with the story "What Lives in a Shell?" by Kathleen Weidner Zoehfeld. The story discusses where different animals live and what types of creatures live in shells. It presents beautiful illustrations of different kinds of shells. Mrs. Doherty has many shell specimens on hand, which are passed around for students to listen to, feel, and smell. Students are encouraged to bring in their own shell specimens from home and share them with the class.

Students also read storybooks such as *Amos and Boris* by William Steig, *Swimmy* by Leo Lionni, and *Is This a House for Hermit Crab?* by Megan McDonald. They also use Scholastic's computer program *The Magic School Bus Explores the Ocean* by Joanna Cole and Bruce Degan. Other books, such as *Dolphins at Daybreak* by Mary Pope Osborne and *The Titanic Lost and Found* by Judy Donnelly, are used for small-group reading materials.

After this literary introduction to and observation of sea life, students each choose a sea creature of interest and form hypotheses about the creature. Factual books such as *Action Book of the Sea and Its Marvels* are used by students to gather data on their particular creature and then write reports, short stories, and poems about the creature. A field trip to a sea life exhibit adds to student excitement about their projects and provides visual and physical information for them to use. Having gathered and analyzed the data, students present their conclusions by producing displays

Figure 4.2 Kindergarten Dictation, Carly Gamson, The Fay School, Houston, Texas

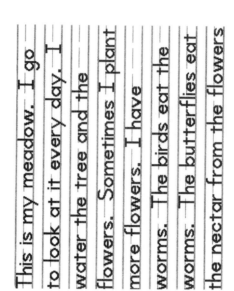

This is my meadow. I go to look at it every day. I water the tree and the flowers. Sometimes I plant more flowers. I have worms. The birds eat the worms. The butterflies eat the nectar from the flowers

which include their reports, their stories, hand-drawn and computer-drawn pictures, and objects such as real fish, pieces of coral, shells, sand, seawater, and seaweed that are related to their creature. Parents and other classes from the school are invited in for a day to visit each display and listen to students deliver their reports and information orally.

Example 3: Natural Phenomena, Myths, and Legends for Fifth and Sixth Graders

Myths, fables, and legends make an excellent start to the study of natural phenomena in fifth- and sixth-grade classes. To begin observing natural phenomena, students can read fables from Aesop, Native American legends, or folklore tales from around the world, which are told in order to explain different natural phenomena. Numerous collections and examples are readily available at the library and online.

Having read these tales, students should be encouraged to form hypotheses about the actual scientific explanations for certain natural phenomena. Once students have read the literary explanations, they should gather data by reading the actual scientific explanations and watching videos which demonstrate the phenomena they have observed in literature and now observe in scientific form. Students can use science texts or other books such as *Risky Business: Storm Chaser—Into the Eye of the Hurricane* by Keith Greenberg, *101 Things Every Kid Should Know About Science* by Samantha Beres, or *Weather* by Robin Kerrod, which include explanations of natural phenomena. Students can research different topics and, after analyzing the data, present their conclusions to the class.

As a part of these presentations to the class, help students find ways of demonstrating their particular phenomenon and its causes. For example, to mimic a hurricane, a student can whirl a length of string with a very large, heavy button attached to one end. The student will notice the faster he whirls the string the more the button seems to pull away from him. The cause is, of course, centrifugal force, which is also the cause of winds in a hurricane pulling away from the center and creating an "eye" (Mandel, 1991). To follow up on the literature, after all the students have presented

(text continues on page 60)

Form 4.6 Some Integrated Elements and Assessment Tips for "Science Is Sensory"

Lesson	Language Arts	Math	Social Studies	Technology	Arts Plus: Art, Drama, Music, PE	Assessment Tips and Other Notes
Make Observations	X		X		X	Reward students for bringing appropriate samples; assess charts based on specificity with which they are completed, age appropriateness, and so on; use composition evaluation sheet (Form 2.2) to evaluate steps in the writing process; assess short stories using prerequisites given to students at beginning of assignment, such as vocabulary usage, punctuation, capitalization, plot, and characterization; assess comparison chart based on accuracy of information provided; use group participation. Have students complete an evaluation similar to the Critics' Choice or Writing Final Assessment (both are in the Appendix).

						Notes
Form a Hypothesis	X					Reward students for providing thoughtful, reasonable responses on the Data Table (Form 4.4).
Gather Data; Analyze the Data	X					Use participation guidelines in Form 2.2.
Draw Conclusions	X					Reward students for thoughtful conclusions (see Form 4.5).
Kindergartners in the Meadow	X		X	X	X	See all notes in this column.
Sea Life in Second Grade	X		X	X	X	See all notes in this column.
Natural Phenomena, Myths, and Legends for Fifth and Sixth Graders	X		X	X	X	See all notes in this column.

their reports, have them choose another phenomenon and create their own tales explaining the existence of that phenomenon.

During the time that the class is studying natural phenomena, take time out of the day to take the class outside or at least to look out the window. Ask the students to keep a "sky journal" in which they record all the interesting things they see (cloud formations, birds, bugs, the sun) during a 5-minute observation of the sky.

Ideas for integrating elements and assessment for lessons in this chapter can be found in Form 4.6 (pages 58-59).

SUMMARY

The five steps of the scientific process, observing, gathering data, forming hypotheses, analyzing data, and drawing conclusions, should be incorporated into any science instruction. By using these steps as a guide for the lesson, you help students learn scientific thinking as a part of reading and writing. Not only are their language and science skills developed but also their critical thinking skills are developed across the curriculum.

RESOURCES

Action Publishing. (1997). *Action Book of the Sea and Its Marvels.* Ocala, FL: Author. Factual book for sea life reports; Grades 2 and 3.

Ada, Alma Flor. (2000). *Friend Frog.* New York: Scholastic. About a field mouse looking for a friend and all the things he encounters along the way—ponds, forests, animal friends; for kindergarten.

Arnold, Eric. (1997). *Volcanoes, Mountains of Fire.* New York: Random House. Discusses eruption of Mount St. Helens and causes of volcanic eruptions; Grade 4.

Beres, Samantha. (1998). *101 Things Every Kid Should Know About Science.* New York: Lowell. Reviews key science concepts in physics, biology, and chemistry; Grades 4, 5, and 6.

Cole, Joanna, & Degan, Bruce. (1995). *Scholastic's The Magic School Bus Explores the Ocean* [Computer software]. Redmond, WA: Microsoft. Software program; Grades 1 and 2.

Donnelly, Judy. (1987). *The Titanic Lost, and Found.* New York: Random House. Factual book for sea life reports; Grades 2 and 3.

Galdone, Paul. (1986). *Over in the Meadow.* New York: Simon & Schuster. An adaptation of the old counting story; for kindergarten.

Greenberg, Keith. (1998). *Risky Business: Storm Chaser—Into the Eye of a Hurricane.* Woodbridge, CT: Blackbirch. About a pilot who flies into the eyes of hurricanes for forecasting data; Grade 6.

Kerrod, Robin. (1998). *Weather.* Milwaukee, WI: Gareth Stevens. Weather facts and activities, explains forces that cause weather; Grade 6.

Lionni, Leo. (1985). *Frederick's Fables.* New York: Pantheon. Stories about sea life; Grades 1 and 2.

Lionni, Leo. (1987). *Fish Is Fish.* New York: Knopf. Swimmy is the only black fish in a school of red ones. After he becomes the lone survivor in the group, he devises a way to protect new friends; Grades 1 and 2.

Lionni, Leo. (1991). *Swimmy.* New York: Knopf. A modern fable about a minnow who wants to follow his tadpole friend turned frog onto land; Grades 1 and 2.

MacDonald, Megan. (1990). *Is This a House for Hermit Crab?* New York: Orchard Books. A story about sea life; Grades 1 and 2.

Mandell, Muriel. (1991). *Simple Weather Experiments With Everyday Materials.* New York: Sterling. Many experiments for Grades 5 and 6.

Osborne, Mary Pope. (1997). *Dolphins at Daybreak.* New York: Scholastic. Factual book for sea life reports; Grades 2 and 3.

Penner, Lucille Recht. (1996). *Twisters.* New York: Random House. Describes, tornadoes, waterspouts, dust devils, and more—and the damage they can cause; Grades 3 and 4.

Rogers, Daniel. (1989). *Weather.* New York: Marshall Cavendish. For Grades 5 and 6.

Steig, William. (1971). *Amos and Boris.* New York: Scholastic. A story about sea life; Grades 1 and 2.

Tarrant, Graham. (1984). *Honeybees.* New York: Putnam. A pop-up book about honeybees, hives, colonies, honeycombs, larvae, and other things; for kindergarten.

The Earth. (1992). New York: Dorling Kindersley. A "picturepedia" with graphics and written explanations for use in earth science; for Grades 3 and 4.

Whyman, Kathryn. (1989). *Hands On Science: Rainbows to Lasers.* New York: Gloucester. Experiments to use with students; Grades 4, 5, and 6.

Zoehfeld, Kathleen Weidner. (2001). "What Lives in a Shell?" In J. David Cooper and John J. Pikulski (Eds.), *Friends* (pp. 125-150). Dallas, TX: Houghton Mifflin. The second-grade text is from the series *Invitations to Literacy*.

CHAPTER FIVE

Social Studies Becomes an Enduring Fabric

The real voyage of discovery consists not in seeking new landscapes, but in having new eyes.

—Marcel Proust

The elementary social studies curriculum is an introduction to the institutions and organizations created by society. In K-1, students learn about themselves and their families, their school and community. As students mature and awareness expands, studies include city, county, state, national, and international matters—all with a view toward the promotion of civic competence so that students are able to assume the "office of citizen," as Thomas Jefferson called it (National Council for the Social Studies [NCSS], 1994, p. 3).

NCSS emphasizes that as a field of study, social studies may be difficult to define because of its multidisciplinary and interdisciplinary nature. "Two main characteristics, however, distinguish social studies as a field of study: it is designed to promote civic competence; and it is integrative, incorporating many fields of endeavor" (NCSS, 1994, p. 3).

According to NCSS (1994), 10 themes serve as organizing strands for social studies curriculum at every grade level; and curriculum should include experiences that provide for the study of these:

I.   **Culture** (culture and cultural diversity)

II.   **Time, Continuity, and Change** (the ways human beings view themselves in and over time)

III.   **People, Places, and Environments**

IV.   **Individual Development and Identity**

V.   **Individuals, Groups, and Institutions** (interactions among individuals, groups, and institutions)

VI.   **Power, Authority, and Governance** (how people create and change structures of power, authority, and governance)

VII.   **Production, Distribution, and Consumption** (how people organize for the production, distribution, and consumption of goods and services)

VIII.   **Science, Technology, and Society** (the relationships among science, technology, and society)

IX.   **Global Connections** (global connections and interdependence)

X.   **Civic Ideals and Practices** (the ideals, principles, and practices of citizenship in a democratic society) (p. 15)

With these strands as the basis for thematic learning, it is possible for the classroom teacher to develop social studies units using knowledge and skills drawn from all subject areas; and the integrative nature of social studies itself becomes quite evident if you employ the lesson grid (Form 5.1). The examples that appear in other graphics in this chapter demonstrate the types of experiences encouraged by NCSS, and each is adaptable among the various elementary grades. They also demonstrate one of the most important principles of teaching and learning set forth by NCSS, that "classroom interaction focuses on sustained examination of a few important topics rather than superficial coverage of many" (p. 11).

(text continues on page 67)

Form 5.1   Lesson Grid

Integrated Social Studies Strands [Insert lesson title here.]

Note to teacher: Use this grid to cross-reference other content areas with social studies strands.

Strand	Language Arts	Math	Science	Fine Arts (Music, Art, Drama)	Physical Education (Games, Dance)	Other Notes
I. Culture						
II. Time, Continuity, and Change						
III. People, Places, and Environments						
IV. Individual Development and Identity						

(Continued)

Form 5.1 Continued

Strand	Language Arts	Math	Science	Fine Arts (Music, Art, Drama)	Physical Education (Games, Dance)	Other Notes
V. Individuals, Groups, and Institutions						
VI. Power, Authority, and Governance						
VII. Production, Distribution, and Consumption						
VIII. Science, Technology, and Society						
IX. Global Connections						
X. Civic Ideals and Practices						

WEAVING THE STRANDS

Example 1: Early America Revisited—Grades K-3

A Thanksgiving feast concludes the Pilgrim Project at The Fay School, Houston, Texas, where first-grade teacher Gena Lewis hosts what has become an annual tradition for students in Grades 1 through 3. Since she believes that the best way to learn something is through experience, Mrs. Lewis and her students travel back in time to the Pilgrim period.

Beginning map studies are introduced using a large flat map showing the seven continents, major bodies of water, and a compass rose, to understand the Mayflower's voyage. Having used yarn for the prime meridian and for the equator, students then match printed cards to appropriate map locations. Students bake, decorate, and eat edible globes—large cookies with icing to represent water and continents. "The transference of information is very important," says Mrs. Lewis, "and these are ways for young students to begin that process" (personal communication, July 25, 2001).

With the unit extending over 3 weeks, students are transported through their imaginations to the 1620s when there were no electric lights and when clothing and language were very different from today. For a period of time daily, students dress in the clothing of the time and live without modern conveniences. Girls wear long skirts and aprons; boys wear vests, sugar loaf hats, and pants tucked to resemble knickers. Students grind corn, play old-fashioned games, dry apples for the winter, and participate in a number of other classroom activities that acquaint them with life of long ago.

Everything possible is done to create an environment in the classroom. For example, three refrigerator crates "make" a Pilgrim home where a fireplace is used for pretend cooking, shelving displays tools and utensils, and herbs are dried. There are a table to set, various work areas, and a book nook filled with pertinent volumes that tell about this period in history. Students weave on a wooden loom, make apple cider, and write with quill pens. During this time, Mrs. Lewis requests that they speak in the vernacular of those days, using terms like "fare-thee-well" and "good day." Students draw by lot the names of actual Pilgrim children found in material from Plimoth Plantation (Plimoth-on-Web, n.d.) and keep a journal in character. Table 5.1 presents a typical week of November afternoons in Mrs. Lewis's first-grade class.

Table 5.1   Typical Week of November Afternoons in One
Classroom

Monday	Discuss all we know about Pilgrims.
	Video, *Plimoth Plantation Colonial Life*
	(Plimoth-on-Web, n.d.)
Tuesday	Map study. Review 7 continents, 4 oceans.
	Paint maps, finish home.
	Discuss why Pilgrims left England.
Wednesday	Children come dressed in Pilgrim clothes.
	Read "Sarah Morton's Day" (Waters, n.d.) for
	flavor of conversation.
Thursday	Trip on the Mayflower.
	Read "Three Young Pilgrims." (Harness, n.d.)
	Discuss the Mayflower Compact and create a
	classroom compact.
Friday	Open work.
A. Cooking	Cook Johnnycakes and slice apples to dry.
B. Sewing	Make Pilgrim pockets and "cross-stitch" sampler.
C. Carpentry	Make a very simple weaving loom (or borrow one
	from a local historical society).
D. Drama	Students act out work in the home—grind herbs,
	crack nuts, polish brass, shuck and grind corn.

All this becomes a frame for students learning about life in England, the Pilgrims' journey to the new world, the first hard winter, and the first Thanksgiving meal cooked with the help of the Indians. They discover that deer and fish, instead of turkey, most likely were eaten at the feast, which lasted 3 days. Mrs. Lewis believes that "a lot of learning sticks when you do it this way. It is a lead into a love of history" (personal communication, July 25, 2001). See the lesson grid in Form 5.2.

Example 2: Students Around the World—Grades 2, 3, and 4

As an introduction to research, Laurie Dreyfuss, former second-, third-, and fourth-grade teacher now at Herod Elementary School

(text continues on page 71)

Form 5.2   Lesson Grid

Integrated Social Studies Strands Early America Revisited

Note to teacher: Use this grid to cross-reference other content areas with social studies strands.

Strand	Language Arts	Math	Science	Fine Arts (Music, Art, Drama)	Physical Education (Games, Dance)	Other Notes
	Ongoing Discussions					
I. Culture	Speech—vernacular; Journals	Simple carpentry		Pilgrim dress		
II. Time, Continuity, and Change	Same as above		Cooking	Same as above		
III. People, Places, and Environments	Same as above			Same as above		Practical arts, and so on, entertainments
IV. Individual Development and Identity	Same as above					Cooperative work—shuck corn, and so on

(Continued)

Form 5.2 Continued

Strand	Language Arts Ongoing Discussions	Math	Science	Fine Arts (Music, Art, Drama)	Physical Education (Games, Dance)	Other Notes
V. Individuals, Groups, and Institutions	Same as above					
VI. Power, Authority, and Governance	Same as above					Mayflower Compact and classroom compacts—why Pilgrims left England
VII. Production, Distribution, and Consumption	Same as above					Cooperative work—crack nuts, set table, and so on
VIII. Science, Technology, and Society	Same as above		Sailing Mayflower			
IX. Global Connections	Same as above		Geography —maps and continents			
X. Civic Ideals and Practices	Same as above					Mayflower Compact and classroom compacts—why Pilgrims left England

in Houston, Texas, has designed a project to familiarize students with other lands. While the project originated with pre-pared materials, Mrs. Dreyfuss has developed the model over several years with additions and modifications. The countries studied, for example, often are dictated by the availability of appropriate books in the library at a particular grade or reading level. A note goes home to parents informing them about the project, requirements, expectations, and due date.

The project begins with each student drawing the name of a country by lot and writing their own names on their country on a world map. "Somehow the person's name on the map helps to estab-lish responsibility and interest, especially when you can see who's next door—not just which country but which classmate," Mrs. Dreyfuss says (personal communication, July 2, 2001). Individualized country packets are handed out, and the study begins.

The project builds on a number of skills and introduces others. Geography, mapmaking, map reading, writing reports and biographies, developing cultural studies, learning about the currency and economy of a country, and speaking before a group are all included. Form 5.3 establishes the assignment for both students and parents.

Mrs. Dreyfuss has found that students like the choices, and the teacher is able to observe their developing interests. The project usually is planned for 6 to 10 weeks beginning in January or later, because by then, students will have developed enough maturity to handle a long project. This also allows the teacher time to make adaptations based on the previous year's experience.

In the past, biographies included such persons as the Brothers Grimm (Germany) and NBA basketball star Hakeem Olajuwon (Nigeria). In the spirit of period costume, one student came as a mummy. Students baked, ate, and enjoyed cookies using a World War I era recipe. Mount Fuji appeared as a vinegar-baking soda volcano. American macaroni and cheese was prepared and com-pared with the Italian counterpart—pasta and white cheese. Someone assigned Norway did an extra poster on the Vikings. "And no matter what the specifics of the assignment may be, everyone is fascinated with the discovery that fairy tales and folk-tales are so similar the world over," Mrs. Dreyfuss says. "A lasting lesson is just how alike we really are" (personal communication, July 2, 2001). Form 5.4 (page 75) is a lesson grid for this project.

(text continues on page 74)

Form 5.3   Students Around the World

Social Studies Project for Grade _____ [Teacher fills in grade.]

Note to teacher: These activities and the vocabulary section will change with your needs and grade level. Arrange regular meetings with students during the course of the work. This helps them to learn time management skills, and you will be able to monitor progress.

Objective: The student will become familiar with an assigned country through research.

Due: Week of _____. Each student will be assigned a specific day for the presentation.

Students will do the following:

1.   Complete the country packet or study guide given to them by the teacher. [*Note to teacher:* The country packets may be based on prepared, reproducible materials purchased in a teachers' supply store or modified from other materials of your choice.]

2.   Dress in the fashion of the country for your presentation. [*Note to teacher:* Native costumes are not required. Students may choose clothing representative of their countries. Mrs. Dreyfuss says that in the spirit of a modern world, some students dress in their own soccer uniforms; tape across the shirt with the name of the designated country represents the change. Another student assigned Canada dressed "warm."]

(Continued)

Form 5.3 (Continued)

3. Complete any two of the following:

   A. Research a famous person, either modern or historical, from the country, and write a brief biography. [*Note to teacher:* You may want to give specific instructions or specify one characteristic or aspect of the person's life in order to prevent copying verbatim.]

   B. Dance a native dance for your class. [*Note to teacher:* This might include native instruments or music, ballet or interpretive dance, or a folk dance involving the whole class.]

   C. Make a poster about the country.

   D. Make a diorama or other three-dimensional representation of a place of interest found in your country.

   E. Prepare and serve a native food.

Special Notes

1. Do not leave this project for the last minute.

   • You may do more than two of the five activities.

   • Be sure to list all your resources.

   • Put your completed packet in a binder or folder and decorate. Include any brochures, maps, and pictures you have collected.

Resources

Airlines	Local firms with international contacts
Videos	Travel agencies
Newspapers	Consulates

(Continued)

Form 5.3 (Continued)

Banks	Individuals with personal experience
Magazines	Internet
Library	

Selected Vocabulary [*Note to teacher:* These are examples of words you might choose. The definitions can be scaled appropriately to grade level or modified as needed.]

1. inhabitant	one who lives in a certain place
2. exploration	the act of traveling over an unknown area and studying it
3. economy	making the best use of money and goods
4. agriculture	the business of raising crops and livestock; farming
5. manufactured	made by hand or machine, in large amounts
6. employment	a person's work or job

Example 3: Who in Your Family First Came to Your State?—Grades 5 and 6

Many states require the study of state history at some time in elementary school. Primary research is the basis for this family history project where students interview family members to write about them and discover what relative first came to their state. The question, "Who is the first member of your family to come to (name of the state)?" is deceptively simple. The questions posed in Form 5.5 (page 77) are designed to get students started in their research and to cover important points but are in no way intended to limit the interview.

It should be apparent that these questions probably will not be answered at one sitting. Students typically find that they must plan several sessions to cover the information. They also find that some questions have answers—and lead to other questions—while some lead nowhere. The questions are intended to serve as a guide for the subsequent essay or report.

(text continues on page 78)

Form 5.4 Lesson Grid

Integrated Social Studies Strands: Students Around the World

Note to teacher: Use this grid to cross-reference other content areas with social studies strands.

Strand	Language Arts Ongoing Discussions	Math	Science	Fine Arts (Music, Art, Drama)	Physical Education (Games, Dance)	Other Notes
I. Culture Fairy Tales	Research, write, present reports	Calculate distances		Pertaining to the assigned country	Pertaining to the assigned country	
II. Time, Continuity, and Change						
III. People, Places, and Environments	Vocabulary studies					Compare with U.S. customs and methods

(Continued)

75

Form 5.4 Continued

Strand	Language Arts, Ongoing Discussions	Math	Science	Fine Arts (Music, Art, Drama)	Physical Education (Games, Dance)	Other Notes
IV. Individual Development	Same as above					Same as above; study skills
V. Individuals, Groups, and Institutions	Same as above					
VI. Power, Authority, and Governance	Same as above					Government of assigned country
VII. Production, Distribution, and Consumption						
VIII. Science, Technology, and Society	Same as above		"Volcano"			
IX. Global Connections	Same as above		Map studies, geography of the country			
X. Civic Ideals and Practices	Same as above					Compare with U.S.

Form 5.5   Family History Project

Directions to the student: Interview members of your family. Make notes about what you learn. Then write an essay about the first member of your family to come to (name of your state). Here are some good questions to ask.

I.   Who was the first member of our family to come to (name your state)?

   A.   How is he or she related to us?

   B.   When did he or she arrive?

   C.   How did he or she arrive? (Method of travel? By what transportation?)

   D.   Where did he or she come from?

II.   Why did she or he come? (What were the reasons?)

   A.   Did she or he come for freedom?

   B.   Did she or he come because of religion?

   C.   Did she or he come because of politics?

   D.   Did she or he come for adventure?

   E.   Did she or he come for fame and fortune?

   F.   Did she or he come to have a better life for the family?

   G.   Did she or he come because of a job or work?

III.   What was his or her background or previous life?

   A.   What was his or her nationality or ethnicity?

   B.   What education, skills, occupation, or profession did he or she have?

   C.   What food or language was he or she accustomed to?

   D.   What problems did he or she face, and were those problems solved?

   E.   What seemed strange or unfamiliar about the new life?

(Continued)

Form 5.5 (Continued)

IV. What are highlights or special memories this person had?

    A. What things did he or she miss about the former life?

    B. What were the enjoyments of the new life?

    C. What did she or he learn or accomplish in the new life?

V. What differences did she or he find between the old life and the new life?

VI. What have I learned from this project?

This project, used in a study of Texas history, led to fascinating tales and information as family documents in the form of wedding portraits and citizenship papers were unearthed. As students became acquainted with a very personal history, they frequently came to view parents and other relatives with new appreciation.

The teacher should bear in mind that this questionnaire is a guide. The project will develop differently for each student, so the work is highly individualized. It can be set over about 6 weeks, with final evaluation and assessment based on the essay or report; an appropriate visual using maps, photos, family documents, or other available materials; and oral presentation to the class. Form 5.6 is a lesson grid for this project.

Example 4: Study Skills and Learning Styles—All Grades

Organization and study skills can be taught in any subject area and should be well in place before a student leaves elementary school. Social studies provides an excellent opportunity to teach and practice these skills while focusing on student learning styles.

Susan Kahn, MEd, educational therapist with the Clinic for Academic Therapy in Bellaire, Texas, points out that an awareness of individual student learning styles—visual, auditory, or kinesthetic—is very helpful to the teacher. Because most students combine all these styles of learning, incorporating strategies from

(text continues on page 81)

Form 5.6 Lesson Grid

Integrated Social Studies Strands: Coming to Texas

Note to teacher: Use this grid to cross-reference other content areas with social studies strands.

Strand	Language Arts	Math	Science	Fine Arts (Music, Art, Drama)	Physical Education (Games, Dance)	Other Notes
I. Culture	Ongoing Discussions Interview, research, write, present report			Visual component		Organizational and study skills
II. Time, Continuity, and Change	Same as above					As pertains to the individual relative
III. People, Places, and Environments	Same as above		Geography			Same as above

(Continued)

Form 5.6 Continued

Strand	Language Arts Ongoing Discussions	Math	Science	Fine Arts (Music, Art, Drama)	Physical Education (Games, Dance)	Other Notes
IV. Individual Development and Identity	Same as above					Sense of family
V. Individuals, Groups, and Institutions	Same as above					Same as above
VI. Power, Authority, and Governance						
VII. Production, Distribution, and Consumption						
VIII. Science, Technology, and Society						
IX. Global Connections	Interview info					As pertains to the relative
X. Civic Ideals and Practices	Same as above					

each area into the classroom helps all students learn more effectively. Here are some useful tips. Obviously, the teacher has only so much time and energy, but these suggestions may serve as reminders to vary the instruction—not just in social studies but in all instruction.

Visual learners learn best by seeing. They may have difficulty with lectures and prefer to read. To help them learn, use color wherever possible. Devise visualizations; and make and use flash cards, pictures, maps, charts, and webs. Auditory learners learn best by listening. They need to hear material to learn it, and they may have difficulty with reading. To help them learn, read textbooks aloud; ask them to recite; listen to tapes or make your own to regulate the rate of speech; ask them to study and discuss with a partner or in small groups. Kinesthetic or tactile learners learn by doing. These are hands-on learners who need concrete, manipulative materials. To help them learn, provide labs, field trips, and other similar experiences; permit students to move while learning. A length of PVC pipe underneath the desk can be used for footwork while students are seated. Use computers to reinforce touch, and schedule short study periods.

Do not assume that students know the simple techniques required for making flash cards or that they recognize the significance of color coding. You might pair or group students to make flash card sets using index cards. Show them how the system works—a question on one side with its answer or response on the other. Then take a look together at a textbook (very likely the social studies text) that uses different colors to indicate headings and other organizational elements. Show students how to transfer this information from one subject to another by making math facts and science vocabulary flash card sets; use different colors to underline the various parts of speech, for example, in language arts. Frequently emphasize these techniques, among others, within your lessons.

The foregoing strategies will provide variety in the classroom for both teacher and students. Two additional study skills often reinforced through social studies are critical reading and note taking. They are so closely related that they scarcely can be separated. Depending on your students' grade, the recommendations in the following section may be adapted as needed.

Developing Critical Reading and Note Taking

Students must be taught to become active readers; and as they work with a passage, they exercise the analytical skills that are required in all subjects. For demonstration purposes, photocopy one or two short passages from the textbook and give a copy to every student as a worksheet. (They will work directly on this paper since they cannot write in the textbooks.) Before reading the passage together, tell students about the purpose for using this text and your expectations, and briefly discuss the content with them. Lead them into the material by way of this short introduction. Then preview the material with them, pointing out important elements such as the title, boldfaced headings, introduction and summary, graphic and pictorial aids, and new vocabulary.

Now read the material aloud as a group, alternating readers by paragraph, with you also taking part. Look for topic sentences and help students to locate main ideas through discussion. Underline the topic sentence (main idea), indicating to students it may not be the first sentence in the paragraph. If feasible, use numbers to sequence or group the details. Take notice of vocabulary and circle or highlight all new words, perhaps in a particular color. Keep a running list of new words, adding them to similar lists for other subjects. Write a synonym or short definition in the margin next to each word.

Include the main idea of the paragraph or section by paraphrasing, and write this in the margin. Include any or all of these that pertain: cause and effect, fact and opinion, comparison and contrast, questions, definitions that arise, examples, and references to other points of interest. Turn the paraphrase of the main idea into questions, and try to answer them in discussion while covering the text. See Figure 5.1 for an example.

Teach students to write a summary by first listing or visually mapping the ideas. Determine the main theme (thesis) of the passage and write it at the top of the notes. Number the main ideas in the order of importance, and write a summary paragraph. A lesson such as this may be spread over several days, depending on the length of the passage, and becomes the basis for teaching note-taking skills.

Summary skills may be taught to kindergarten students when they are regularly given the opportunity to tell "what we did" in

Figure 5.1 The Pledge of Allegiance as Text for Discussion
Note: Depending on the students' grade level, more incisive questions can be asked. Vocabulary must be addressed, as well as the meaning of this 31-word sentence.

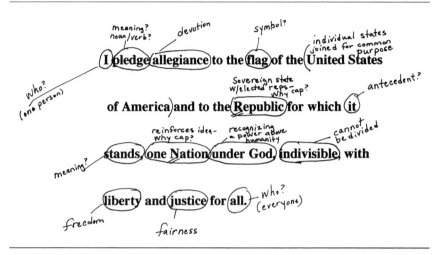

one or two sentences for the teacher to write on the board. Dictation (speech) becomes associated with writing very early when students see their words written. Very soon, students will cast their own summary sentences and write them phonetically. With practice, by the end of first grade, most students are able to write their own short sentences.

This regular use of summary is highly important in helping students to focus and order their thoughts at the end of a lesson. It is a method of providing closure as well as an introductory method of teaching students to take notes and review their work. It leads into progressively more extended work (writing paragraphs and essays) in a gradual fashion and provides regular opportunity for writing in any subject. Form 5.7 is a lesson grid for study skills and learning styles.

SUMMARY

Elementary social studies is an introduction to the institutions and organizations created by society. It is an extremely integrative

(text continues on page 86)

Form 5.7 Lesson Grid

Integrated Social Studies Strands: Study Skills and Learning Styles

Note to teacher: Use this grid to cross-reference other content areas with social studies strands. Choose text from any content area for development of critical thinking and personal responsibility.

Strand	Language Arts	Math	Science	Fine Arts (Music, Art, Drama)	Physical Education (Games, Dance)	Other Notes
Critical Thinking—All Subjects	Ongoing Discussions					
I. Culture						
II. Time, Continuity, and Change						
III. People, Places, and Environments						
IV. Individual Development and Identity	Textual analysis; Critical reading, Vocabulary					Development of organizational and study skills—note taking

V. Individuals, Groups, and Institutions					
VI. Power, Authority, and Governance					
VII. Production, Distribution, and Consumption					
VIII. Science, Technology, and Society					
IX. Global Connections					
X. Civic Ideals and Practices					

subject rich with the opportunity for thematic work using the 10 organizing strands supplied by NCSS. It is possible for ideas and concepts that promote the development of civic competence to take shape in the classroom and for students to participate fully in the process. In-depth work and the development of study skills provide a foundation for student achievement beyond the elementary classroom.

RESOURCES

Chapman, Anne. (Ed.). (1993). *Making Sense: Teaching Critical Reading Across the Curriculum.* New York: College Board.

Frender, Gloria. (1990). *Learning to Learn: Strengthening Study Skills and Brain Power.* Nashville, TN: Incentive Publications.

Harness, Cheryl. (n.d.). *Three Young Pilgrims.* Retrieved July 29, 2002, from www.marketstream.com/acb/index.cfm?DID=12

Hirsch, E. Donald., Jr. (Ed.). (1999). *Core Knowledge Series.* Charlottesville, VA: Core Knowledge Foundation. Seven volumes organized one per grade beginning with *What Your Kindergartner Needs to Know* and ending with *What Your Sixth Grader Needs to Know.*

Irvin, Judith, & Rose, Elaine O. (1995). *Starting Early With Study Skills: A Week-by-Week Guide for Elementary Students.* Needham Heights, MA: Allyn & Bacon.

National Council for the Social Studies. (1994). *Expectations of Excellence: Curriculum Standards for Social Studies.* Washington, DC: Author. Retrieved July 29, 2002, from www.socialstudies.org

Plimoth-on-Web. (n.d.). Plimoth Plantation ™; The Living History Museum of 17th Century Plymouth. Discover a wealth of early American information and suggestions, everything from clothing to looms, subject area bibliographies, books, and videos.

The Mayflower Compact. Retrieved August 9, 2002, from www.plimoth.org/Library/compact.htm; "Mayflower Passengers," retrieved July 31, 2002, from www.plimoth.org/Library/maypass.htm; *Plimoth Plantation Colonial Life,* retrieved July 21, 2002, from www.marketstream.com/acb/index.cfm?DID=12

Proust, Marcel. (n.d.). Retrieved July 31, 2002, from www.chesco.com/~artman/proust.html

Waters, Kate. (n.d.). *Sarah Morton's Day: A Day in the Life of a Pilgrim Girl.* Retrieved July 29, 2002, from www.marketstream.com/acb/index.cfm?DID=12

More Things to Do

Arrange for guest speakers to visit your class.

Contact local heritage museums or other local historical places or organizations for tours, literature, and other forms of help.

Use newspapers, magazines, and other periodicals for information regarding topics and events of interest to the class.

Work with your library media specialist for suggestions regarding the development of thematic units of study. The Internet is always an excellent resource.

CHAPTER SIX

Technology: Getting It Before It Gets Us

Please, let's remember: It's not about how we use the
TOOLS. *It's (mostly) about how we **USE** the tools.*

—Judi Harri (n.d.)

With technology, we may dream about the ideal: a computer in every classroom, a computer lab in the building with state-of-the-art hardware and software, a library media specialist and a library media center with a computerized catalog and plenty of CDs, a technology specialist and high-speed internet connections, televisions and VCRs in every classroom, and calculators for every student. However, the reality may be that older students occasionally come down and use the computers in the computer lab to type already handwritten thank-you letters using word processing software, students sometimes use the computers to practice for standardized tests, and teachers occasionally type tests or worksheets or report cards or check their e-mail for morning announcements from the principal, but really all that technology has not truly enhanced learning. The computers in the classrooms seem to take valuable space that could be used for other things, or the printer never works properly, or the e-mail server is down again, or the technology available really isn't so state-of-the-art after all. The television gets used for recess on rainy days, but there aren't any videos which really integrate with the lessons, and half the calculators don't work. What does all this mean?

Technology integration in the schools requires lots of planning on a schoolwide level and on a classroom level. Coordination between the computer teacher and the regular classroom teacher is essential; everyone must have an understanding that technology is not the end but rather a means—a tool for learning. Use of technology must grow out of regular classroom instruction in order to be valid. Otherwise, students are quite correct when they ask, "Are we going to play on the computers today?" rather than "What are we learning in computer class?" If your school doesn't have all the latest and greatest equipment or a computer teacher or a technology specialist, then obviously, classroom teachers become responsible for the integration of whatever technology is available. Some guidelines for how to proceed are available whether teachers must work alone or with the aid of a technology specialist.

The International Society for Technology in Education (ISTE) (2000) suggests the following standards for schools. While each school must develop its own plan and specific standards and goals, these basic standards for students will probably be included in most plans.

1. Basic operations and concepts

- Demonstrate a sound understanding of the nature and operation of technology systems.
- Become proficient in the use of technology.

2. Social, ethical, and human issues

- Understand the ethical, cultural, and societal issues related to technology.
- Practice responsible use of technology systems, information, and software.
- Develop positive attitudes toward technology uses that support lifelong learning, collaboration, personal pursuits, and productivity.

3. Technology productivity tools

- Use technology tools to enhance learning, increase productivity, and promote creativity.
- Use productivity tools to collaborate in constructing technology-enhanced models, prepare publications, and produce other creative works.

4. Technology communication tools

- Use telecommunications to collaborate, publish, [and] interact with peers, experts, and other audiences.
- Use a variety of media and formats to communicate information and ideas effectively to multiple audiences.

5. Technology research tools

- Use technology to locate, evaluate, and collect information from a variety of sources.
- Use technology tools to process data and report results.
- Evaluate and select new information resources and technological innovations based on appropriateness for specific tasks.

6. Technology problem-solving and decision-making tools

- Use technology resources for solving problems and making informed decisions.
- Employ technology in the development of strategies for solving problems in the real world.

Because most teachers and schools have integrated the use of older forms of technology into the curriculum, the examples which follow apply mainly to the use of computers and computer accessories. Throughout the book, we have provided examples of ways to integrate computer use into subject-specific lessons. Here we provide examples at all grade levels which incorporate specific objectives for technology use while at the same time integrating technology into regular instruction.

KINDERGARTEN AND THE ABCS

A yearlong project which allows students to print a finished product every time they visit the computer lab or use the computer in the classroom involves the students' study of the alphabet—a first step toward learning to read. Have students make letter books on the computer. For every letter they study, they will be learning words that begin with that letter. Choose one word or several and ask students to draw pictures on the computer to illustrate the words. Then have students dictate sentences (which you, the computer teacher, a classroom aide, or older student helper will type) to go along with the pictures they have drawn. Figures 6.1 and 6.2 demonstrate the progression seen from the beginning of the year to the end.

As an introduction, have students type their own names, pointing out that holding the shift key down makes a capital letter and pressing the space bar puts spaces between the words. Help students find the particular keys on the keyboard for which they are looking. All keys on the keyboard are in capitals, which is sometimes confusing to younger students. As the year proceeds, students will move from simply stating random thoughts about the pictures they have drawn to creating more complex sentences and stories. Such activity reinforces language development and emphasizes that computers are used as part of the work we do. Box 6.1 summarizes technology standards achieved through these activities.

While kindergarten students will produce and print a piece each time they work at the computer, the following projects for students in Grades 1 through 5 are designed to be done over a long period of time—anywhere from 9 weeks to a semester. Students will not print every time they work on the project but will print once or twice to proofread and revise. A final copy will be printed upon completion of the entire project.

FIRST GRADE—ALL ABOUT ME

In first grade, students are very curious about the world around them but, for the most part, still see everything only as it relates to them or affects them. A perfect project to begin the year is to have students develop pages for a book about themselves, a project many teachers do but which can be enhanced using the computer. Discuss with students those things that they might like to include in a book and, as a group, make a list of these ideas for

(text continues on page 94)

Figure 6.1 Dinosaurs by Jacqueline Jacobs, Kindergarten, The Fay School, Houston, Texas

tricerotops

T. Rex

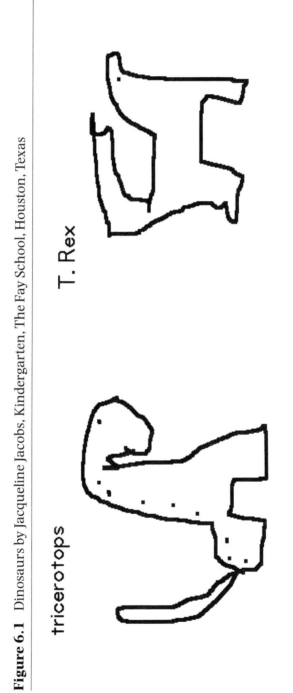

Figure 6.2   Vegetables by Calin Ackerman, Kindergarten, The
            Fay School, Houston, Texas

Once upon a time, there
was vegetables. A little girl
hated vegetables. She
tried a carrot. She didn't
like it. She tried corn. She
didn't like it. She tried
broccoli. It tasted good!
The End.

Box 6.1   Technology Standards Achieved in Kindergarten and the ABCs

---

1. **Basic operations and concepts: Students are proficient in the use of technology**. Students learn the parts of the computer and what each will do. Eye-hand coordination is developed as students draw with the mouse. Simple keyboarding is reinforced through regular reminders, such as using the shift key to make capital letters when students type their names on their work.

2. **Technology productivity tools: Students use technology tools to enhance learning, increase productivity, and promote creativity**. Creating letter books by drawing pictures and writing stories enhances language development and encourages creativity while integrating computer use into regular instruction.

3. **Technology productivity tools: Students use productivity tools to collaborate in constructing technology-enhanced models, prepare publications, and produce other creative works**. Students complete a letter book each week by drawing and then dictating their ideas or stories. They must make choices about the graphics tools to use. They observe and participate in typing, thus beginning to develop keyboarding skills while also practicing reading skills as they see their dictated words appear on the screen. Students have a publication to share with classmates and parents, reinforcing language development and providing an opportunity to hear new ideas for continued work.

---

student-produced artwork and dictation—produced on the computer: for example, pictures of themselves, their family and pets, their home, their favorite food, their best friend, and their teacher. They might also want to incorporate into their computer artwork action pictures of favorite games or other activities. This list is not complete. There will be other items that are of interest and importance to the students.

After the list has been developed, ask students to begin by drawing on the computer a picture of themselves. Once the picture is complete, students may dictate (or type themselves if they have developed some proficiency) what they would like to tell about who they are. Encourage students to dictate sentences which give their names, their ages, and descriptions of themselves and their families. See Figure 6.3 (page 96) for an example from an autobiography.

Save the day's work on a disk or on the computer hard drive, so each time students use the computer, they continue the project, creating multiple drawings and dictations in their autobiographies. When students feel they have completed their books, print all the pages, arrange them in the proper order, and then bind them by punching holes in the pages and tying them with ribbon for the students to take home. Box 6.2 (page 97) summarizes technology standards achieved through these drawing and dictation activities in which students learn to manipulate the mouse and use graphics software.

SECOND GRADE—PANCAKES AND COMPUTERS

In second grade, an interesting way to enhance keyboarding skills and to teach students about proper formatting when they write is to use a picture book as a prompt for students to write and illustrate their own stories. This project also provides excellent opportunities for proofreading and shows students how easy it is to make revisions on the computer.

Begin with a book such as *Pancakes for Breakfast* by Tomie dePaola. This book has few words; and the pictures have very few colors, leaving much to the imagination of the students. Show students the book and read aloud with them, asking them to fill in the story as you go through the pages.

When they are ready to begin their stories, show students the important keys which they may need to use on the keyboard—where the comma and period keys are, how to make an exclamation mark, and that using the tab key will automatically indent the same number of spaces for a new paragraph every time. Demonstrate that most word processing programs automatically move the text to the next line of the page when necessary. Second grade is also a good age to give students their own disks and to

Figure 6.3   *All About Me* by Mollie Gaylor, First Grade, The Fay
School, Houston, Texas

This is me. This is a
beautiful day. I just got
home from school. I'm
going to Lane's house. I'm
gona play with Ginger and
Scoobie. Ginger has white
fur and his ears are kinda
brownish black and

Box 6.2   Technology Standards Achieved in First Grade—All About Me

---

1. **Basic operations and concepts: Students are proficient in the use of technology.** Students develop greater eye-hand coordination while making drawings on the computer; they also begin more intensive use of the keyboard and begin learning key positions. They develop skills opening and closing software and saving their work and reopening it from week to week or day to day.

2. **Social, ethical, and human issues: Students develop a positive attitude toward technology use that supports lifelong learning, collaboration, personal pursuits, and productivity.** Students enjoy the project because they are allowed to tell whatever is important to them. While they are making the books, students share their ideas with others and hear what others have to say about the writing. Students produce a final product which they may share with their classmates and their families.

3. **Technology productivity tools: Students use productivity tools to collaborate in constructing technology-enhanced models, prepare publications, and produce other creative works.** By creating and publishing books about themselves, students easily see many uses for the computer without having to learn new subject matter. Students also make choices about which graphic tools are the best for their purposes and thus develop skills with several computer tools.

---

teach them how to insert and eject them properly. You will also need to explain the steps for opening work saved to a disk and for saving work to a disk as required by your software. Students will have to follow these steps each time they work on the project.

With all this information, students are now ready to write their own stories using the book and its illustrations to help them develop their ideas. First, ask students to design a title or cover page. Show students how to center text and how to change fonts and font sizes until they have the page they want. Next, students should write and illustrate their stories. For each page or two of text (which may consist of one or two sentences each), have students make an illustration. At the end of the book, have students make an About the Author page in which they provide autobiographical information. They may either draw a picture of themselves or use the scanner to add a photograph of themselves to the page. If you do not have access to a scanner and want to include photographs, you may wish to demonstrate another type of technology—the copy machine. Simply attach the photo to the printed page with the autobiographical information and make a copy to put at the end of the book. Figure 6.4 is an example from a finished book.

Once students have printed their books, bind them by punching holes in the paper and using yarn or ribbon to tie the pages together or by using the plastic spiral bind combs. Showing students how to use the spiral-binding machine provides yet another example of technology for students to learn. Box 6.3 (page 100) summarizes technology standards achieved through these activities.

THIRD GRADE—FAMILY ALBUM

Third-grade students are developing an interest in those around them, particularly family members. To make the most of this interest, tell students they are going to create family albums in which they provide biographical information and pictures— either drawings or photographs—about their families (this can include extended families and pets if the students choose). Send a note home to parents asking them to provide information about each member of the family, such as date and place of birth, occupation, hobbies, place of residence, and interesting tidbits. Ideally, students will write this information as their parents talk to them about each person. Also ask parents to send photographs of family members or pets if at all possible.

Begin by reviewing formatting with students. Show them how to center text, change fonts and font sizes, and so forth. Also show students how to incorporate software graphics into their work. Allow students to design cover pages for their books which include a title, the author's name, and a representative graphic.

Figure 6.4   From *The Cold Cooking* by Taylor Mattingly, Second
Grade, The Fay School, Houston, Texas

Once upon a time there was a street called
Pancake Street. Everybody made pancakes with syrup.

Next have students write a short biography about each member of the family, using the information obtained from their
parents. For students with very large families, you may wish to limit
this to five family members—although all members will be named.
Remind students to capitalize sentences, to put one space after a
comma and two spaces after a period or other ending punctuation
mark. Have students create a separate page for each member of the
family to allow room for a drawing or photograph to go with each
biography. Students should provide all text first so that proofreading and revision can take place. Demonstrate the use of spell
checker, informing students that the computer only recognizes
misspelled words and not correctly spelled words that are misused.

Once the text has been proofread and revised, help students
add drawings and photographs to their pages using graphics elements of the software or using the scanner. Figure 6.5 (page 101)
is a page from a finished book.

Box 6.3   Technology Standards Achieved in Second Grade—Pancakes and Computers

---

1. **Basic operations and concepts: Students demonstrate a sound understanding of the nature and operation of technology systems.** By learning how to insert disks, to save work to a disk, and to retrieve work from a disk, students develop a broader understanding of how computers actually work.

2. **Basic operations and concepts: Students are proficient in the use of technology.** Students greatly increase their knowledge of word processing programs, learning formatting and keyboarding skills.

3. **Social, ethical, and human issues: Students practice responsible use of technology systems, information, and software.** Students must learn to take care of the disks and how to save to and retrieve information from these disks. Students who do not pay attention to the details of these lessons often find that they have lost work or produced work which is not what they had hoped it would be.

4. **Technology productivity tools: Students use technology tools to enhance learning, increase productivity, and promote creativity.** Using a scanner demonstrates to students ways in which to incorporate different media into their own work; using a copy machine helps students incorporate another form of technology into their projects.

Print the books and bind them for students to take home. In addition, if your school has a projector or large monitor connected to one of the computers, students may wish to invite their parents to school to see a presentation of the family albums. All students should operate the computer which projects their

Figure 6.5   Family Album Page by Eric van Doesburg, Third
Grade, The Fay School, Houston, Texas

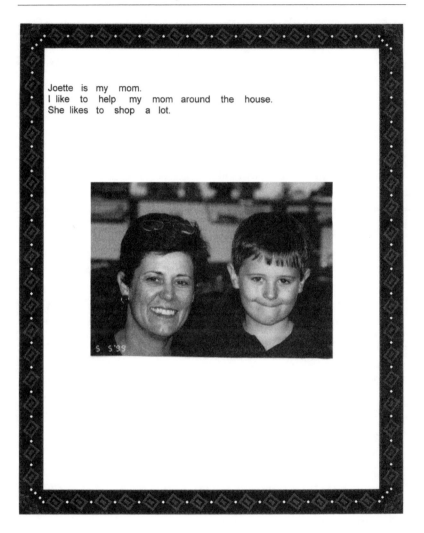

documents on the screen. They should place the disk into the
computer, access the appropriate document, open it, and advance
each page of their albums while delivering a monologue on the work.
If your school has software which actually reads aloud what
students have written and allows the addition of sound to presentations, you may wish to show students how to incorporate these
elements into their albums. Then during the presentations, the

---

Box 6.4   Technology Standards Achieved in Third Grade—Family Album

---

1. **Basic operations and concepts: Students demonstrate a sound understanding of the nature and operation of technology systems.** By the completion of the family albums, students are rather comfortable with the use of technology, from saving to disks to scanning photographs into their written work.

3. **Technology productivity tools: Students use technology to enhance learning, increase productivity, and promote creativity.** Students enhance their knowledge of their families by using information gathered from their parents and by using technology to create a book based on that information.

4. **Technology communication tools: Students use a variety of media and formats to communicate information and ideas effectively to multiple audiences.** Students use a scanner and projection equipment to present their albums in both written and oral formats.

---

computer software would actually read the biographies the students have written while photographs and text are displayed on the projection screen. You may also wish to invite students in other grades to the presentations.

Note: Don't underestimate the power of families here. Many students have parents, older siblings, or other family members who have expertise and access to equipment. Get help wherever you can.

Box 6.4 summarizes technology standards achieved through these activities.

FOURTH GRADE—GOING ON A TRIP

One way to incorporate technology into a project is to have students design a travel brochure for a particular city. This can be a project tied to social studies, math, science, and language arts.

Begin by showing students travel brochures from different cities. Talk about the information provided in these brochures: average temperatures, tourist attractions, lodging and restaurants, and maps of the city. Have students research the city and gather information they might use. Research can be done on the Internet, at a travel agency, or in the library. When using the Internet for research, it is a good idea to bookmark specific sites ahead of time, so students can access the sites and gather the information they need. Show students how to copy and paste information from the Web site to the word processing program so they can use the information after putting it in their own words. Also show them ways to copy and paste graphics they may want to use. Students need to provide a Works Cited list on their brochure giving credit to the sources they used to gather the information. Students should make note of sources or print or copy this information to keep in a folder.

Next, have students design a layout for their brochure. One easy way to help them to format is to show them how to use a three-column layout, which is generally a part of any word processing package. Again, emphasize proper formatting, spacing, spelling, and sentence structure. Once students have gathered their information, they should place it in the brochure they have designed. If they have photographs they wish to use, help them paste (using the copy and paste commands on the computer) or scan the photographs into their work. See Figure 6.6 (page 104) for a rough draft of a brochure.

When students have finished, have them print the final brochure. If you have a duplexing printer, students can easily print on each side of a page and have the brochure look like an actual travel brochure. If you do not have such a printer, show students how to manually print on both sides. Finally, students should present their completed brochures to the class. Box 6.5 (page 105) summarizes technology standards achieved through these activities.

FIFTH AND SIXTH GRADES—THE SCHOOL NEWSPAPER AND WEB SITE

Once students have reached fifth or sixth grade, they have developed enough independence to work on projects in and out of the classroom. They are more aware of their surroundings and occurrences in the outside world. Having students create a school newspaper allows them to collaborate with each other, to do

Figure 6.6 Sample Rough Draft of Brochure, Thomas Deskin and Graham Gaylor, Fourth Grade, The Fay School, Houston, Texas

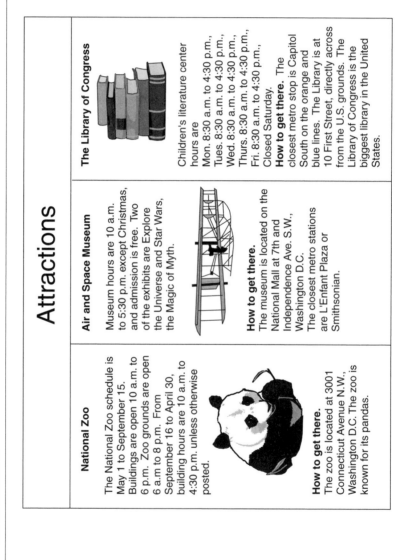

Attractions

National Zoo

The National Zoo schedule is May 1 to September 15. Buildings are open 10 a.m. to 6 p.m. Zoo grounds are open 6 a.m to 8 p.m. From September 16 to April 30, building hours are 10 a.m. to 4:30 p.m. unless otherwise posted.

How to get there.
The zoo is located at 3001 Connecticut Avenue N.W., Washington D.C. The zoo is known for its pandas.

Air and Space Museum

Museum hours are 10 a.m. to 5:30 p.m. except Christmas, and admission is free. Two of the exhibits are Explore the Universe and Star Wars, the Magic of Myth.

How to get there.
The museum is located on the National Mall at 7th and Independence Ave. S.W., Washington D.C.
The closest metro stations are L'Enfant Plaza or Smithsonian.

The Library of Congress

Children's literature center hours are
Mon. 8:30 a.m. to 4:30 p.m., Tues. 8:30 a.m. to 4:30 p.m., Wed. 8:30 a.m. to 4:30 p.m., Thurs. 8:30 a.m. to 4:30 p.m., Fri. 8:30 a.m. to 4:30 p.m., Closed Saturday.
How to get there. The closest metro stop is Capitol South on the orange and blue lines. The Library is at 10 First Street, directly across from the U.S. grounds. The Library of Congress is the biggest library in the United States.

Box 6.5   Technology Standards Achieved in Fourth Grade—Going on a Trip

---

2. **Social, ethical, and human issues: Students understand the ethical, cultural, and societal issues related to tech-nology.** Having students document the sources of information used in their brochures helps them understand the importance of giving credit to the original authors of the work and is a first step toward understanding the seriousness of plagiarism.

5. **Technology research tools: Students use technology to locate, evaluate, and collect information from a variety of sources.** Students use the Internet, electronic media, and other resources available in the library. They are able to make comparisons and selections from a variety of resources.

5. **Technology research tools: Students use technology tools to process data and report results.** After collecting information from a variety of sources, students must assemble the information into a useable format to create their brochures.

5. **Technology research tools: Students evaluate and select new information resources and technological innovations based on appropriateness for specific tasks.** Students choose information from their sources which best meets the needs of the project.

6. **Technology problem-solving and decision-making tools: Students employ technology in the development of strategies for solving problems in the real world.** Figuring out how to print their brochures correctly is a task which calls for students to use problem-solving skills to get the desired results.

---

research, and to publish and distribute their work to the entire school. If your school has a Web site, students may also be able to link to that Web site and present their work to the outside world.

Begin by looking at actual newspapers and their layout, including modest local papers. Point out to students that most large newspapers put national and international news on the front page along with any news about the city which is important. The first section of the paper usually includes news from around the world. Subsequent sections provide news about the city, entertainment, and sports. Ask students to decide what kind of information they wish to include in their paper. Will it just include school news or do they wish to include news from the outside world? Are they going to write about individual classes? Should they have an interview with the principal? Finally, ask them to come up with a name for the paper.

Once these decisions have been made, assign students (you may wish to have them work in pairs at first) to particular articles and help them decide how to proceed. Students should develop questions for interviews and either go to the various classrooms to interview the particular individuals (they may wish to use a tape recorder to get all the information needed), or, if your school has an e-mail system, e-mail the questions to the individual. If particular classes are doing scientific experiments or social studies projects, students may wish to use the Internet to research other similar experiments and their results or the historical applications of the social studies projects. Students should take applicable pictures with either a regular or digital camera (if available), or find pictures on the Internet or in the library.

Once all the information has been gathered, students should write their articles and turn them in for proofreading and revision. When the final revisions have been made, begin by printing a page with layout but no text, divided for the masthead and three columns, as provided by your software. Have students physically cut and paste their articles and pictures (you may wish to use copies made on the copy machine so as not to damage original prints) to fit into the layout. If there is too much information for one issue of the paper, involve students in making decisions about which articles to shorten or cut altogether and which to keep. When this is completed, demonstrate for students how to move their articles and pictures into the layout on the computer. See Figure 6.7 for an example of the first page of a fifth-grade newspaper.

Once the layout is complete, print a copy and give it to the principal or another responsible party for proofreading and revision. Make sure that students are aware of this step and understand that only such a person can give permission for the school to publish the paper. This step ensures that no information is published which is not in accordance with school policy. Print as many copies as necessary and distribute them to the students and teachers. At this time, you

Figure 6.7   Sample First Page of Newspaper—Fifth Grade—The Fay School, Houston, Texas

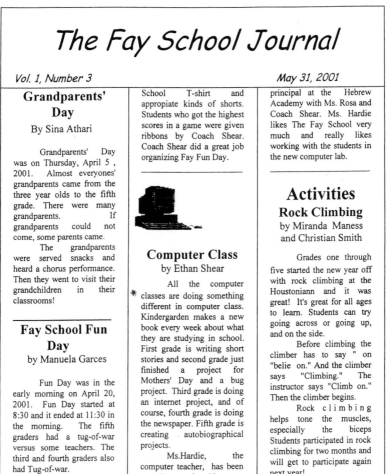

The Fay School Journal

Vol. 1, Number 3   May 31, 2001

Grandparents' Day

By Sina Athari

Grandparents' Day was on Thursday, April 5, 2001. Almost everyones' grandparents came from the three year olds to the fifth grade. There were many grandparents. If grandparents could not come, some parents came.

The grandparents were served snacks and heard a chorus performance. Then they went to visit their grandchildren in their classrooms!

Fay School Fun Day

by Manuela Garces

Fun Day was in the early morning on April 20, 2001. Fun Day started at 8:30 and it ended at 11:30 in the morning. The fifth graders had a tug-of-war versus some teachers. The third and fourth graders also had Tug-of-war.

For Fun Day everyone wore The Fay

School T-shirt and appropiate kinds of shorts. Students who got the highest scores in a game were given ribbons by Coach Shear. Coach Shear did a great job organizing Fay Fun Day.

Computer Class

by Ethan Shear

All the computer classes are doing something different in computer class. Kindergarden makes a new book every week about what they are studying in school. First grade is writing short stories and second grade just finished a project for Mothers' Day and a bug project. Third grade is doing an internet project, and of course, fourth grade is doing the newspaper. Fifth grade is creating autobiographical projects.

Ms.Hardie, the computer teacher, has been an educator for 25 years. Previously, she was

principal at the Hebrew Academy with Ms. Rosa and Coach Shear. Ms. Hardie likes The Fay School very much and really likes working with the students in the new computer lab.

Activities
Rock Climbing
by Miranda Maness and Christian Smith

Grades one through five started the new year off with rock climbing at the Houstoniann and it was great! It's great for all ages to learn. Students can try going across or going up, and on the side.

Before climbing the climber has to say " on "belie on." And the climber says "Climbing." The instructor says "Climb on." Then the climber begins.

Rock climbing helps tone the muscles, especially the biceps Students participated in rock climbing for two months and will get to participate again next year!

****

Box 6.6   Technology Standards Achieved in Grades 5 and 6—School Newspaper and Web Site

---

4. **Technology communication tools: Students use telecommunications to collaborate, publish, and interact with peers, experts, and other audiences.** Students use e-mail to interact with teachers and peers; they use the Internet to research information for articles, and in the process learn the value of telecommunications tools.

4. **Technology communications tools: Students use a variety of media and formats to communicate information and ideas effectively to multiple audiences.** By using regular and digital cameras, scanners, and a Web site, students become fully involved in, and familiar with, the uses of communications tools.

6. **Technology problem-solving and decision-making tools: Students employ technology in the development of strategies for solving problems in the real world.** Creating a school newspaper and Web site link encourages students to solve problems they will encounter in the real world. Problems must be viewed objectively and handled in a manner which is most beneficial to all involved.

---

should also publish the paper on your Web site, if possible. Box 6.6 summarizes technology standards achieved through these activities.

OTHER SUGGESTIONS FOR PROJECTS

Students can improve their computer skills in numerous ways. For example, use formula poems where students must follow directions line by line to teach students formatting skills (see the Appendix for an example). Work with a teacher at a different school to provide e-mail pen pals for students. Have students draw pictures and label the parts of sea creatures, insects, or other creatures as a part of long-term projects in which they are involved in the regular class-room (see the Appendix for an example); or work with the art

(text continues on page 116)

Form 6.1   Integrated Elements and Assessment Tips

Some Integrated Elements and Assessment Tips

Lesson	Language Arts	Math	Science	Social Studies	Arts Plus: Art, Drama, Music, PE	Assessment Tips and Other Notes
Kindergarten and the ABCs	X	X	X	X	X	Assess students as year progresses, based on improving eye-hand coordination, ability to listen and follow instructions, willingness to try new tools, increasing keyboarding skills, etc. These lessons also provide an excellent opportunity for assessing language development and retention of information in a variety of subject areas. Reward students for creativity and willingness to experiment appropriately.

(Continued)

Form 6.1 Continued

Lesson	Language Arts	Math	Science	Social Studies	Arts Plus: Art, Drama, Music, PE	Assessment Tips and Other Notes
First Grade—All About Me	X	X	X	X	X	Assess students as year progresses, based on improving eye-hand coordination, ability to listen and follow instructions, willingness to try new tools, increasing keyboarding skills, etc. Also, evaluate students' ability to perform tasks such as opening and closing software programs and navigating to the correct part of the program for the assignment. Observe students' development in choosing specific graphics tools to perform the jobs they are working on. These lessons also provide an excellent opportunity for assessing language development and retention of information in a variety of subject areas. Reward students for creativity

					and imagination. Praise students for learning information about software and computers beyond the scope of a specific lesson.
				X	Assess students during course of lesson completion, based on increasingly complex use of technological hardware, media, and software programs, formatting of published work, keyboarding skills. This lesson also provides an excellent opportunity for assessing language development and retention of information in a variety of subject areas. Reward students for creativity and imagination. Praise students for
			X		
		X			
	X				
Second Grade— Pancakes and Computers	X				

(Continued)

Form 6.1 Continued

Lesson	Language Arts	Math	Science	Social Studies	Arts Plus: Art, Drama, Music, PE	Assessment Tips and Other Notes
						learning information about software and computers beyond the scope of a specific lesson.
Third Grade—Family Album	X	X	X	X	X	Assess students during course of lesson completion, based on increasingly complex use of technological hardware, media, and software programs, formatting of published work, keyboarding skills. This lesson also provides an excellent opportunity for assessing language development and retention of information in a variety of subject areas. Reward students for creativity and imagination. Praise students for learning information about software and

112

Fourth Grade— Going on a Trip	X	X	X	X	X	computers beyond the scope of a specific lesson. Assess students during course of lesson completion, based on increasingly complex use of technological hardware, media, and software programs, use of research tools, formatting of published work, keyboarding skills. Assess students' problem-solving skills by observing them as they format their works for publication. This lesson also provides an excellent opportunity for assessing language development, research skills, listening skills, and retention of information in a variety of subject areas. Reward students for creativity and imagination.

(Continued)

Form 6.1 Continued

Lesson	Language Arts	Math	Science	Social Studies	Arts Plus: Art, Drama, Music, PE	Assessment Tips and Other Notes
						Praise students for learning information about software and computers beyond the scope of a specific lesson.
Fifth and Sixth Grades— The School Newspaper and Web Site	X	X	X	X	X	Assess students during course of lesson completion based on increasingly complex use of technological hardware (digital cameras, scanners, video cameras), media, and software programs, use of research tools, formatting of published work, keyboarding skills. Assess students' problem-solving skills by observing them as they

format their works for publication. This lesson also provides an excellent opportunity for assessing language development, research skills, listening skills, interviewing skills, and retention of information in a variety of subject areas.

Reward students for creativity and imagination.

Praise students for learning information about software and computers beyond the scope of a specific lesson.

teacher to create collages using pictures drawn on the computer and then printed in multiples. Ask students who soon will be graduating from the school to produce autobiographical presentations with text, sound, and graphics—which can be presented to parents and students in other classes.

SUMMARY

All the lessons in this chapter were devised and taught in concert with the classroom teacher. Students worked once a week in a computer lab with a technology specialist. Although not all schools have access to labs and specialists, in order for students to understand how technology can enhance their work, such technology must be incorporated into the regular curriculum. Students must use technology in real-world situations which will enable them to see many possible applications beyond typing papers and playing games. Long-term projects enable the teacher to incorporate many different aspects of computer and computer-accessory use into lessons while giving students the opportunity to produce fine published pieces. Such projects also promote critical and extended thinking. See Form 6.1 (pages 109-115) for examples of integrated elements and assessment.

RESOURCES

dePaola, Tomie. (1978). *Pancakes for Breakfast.* New York: Harcourt Brace Jovanovich.

Harris, Judi. (n.d.). Teacher Tools @2Learn.ca. Retrieved August 1, 2002, from www.2learn.ca/TeacherTools/teachertools.html.

International Society for Technology in Education. (2000). Address: 1787 Agate Street, Eugene, OR 97403-1923. Retrieved July 30, 2002, from cnets.iste.org

Software Programs

Bytes of Learning. (2000). *UltraKey* (Version 4.0). A good program for self-paced keyboarding instruction. Markham, Ontario, Canada: Author.

Davidson and Associates. (1995). *KidWorks Deluxe* [Computer software]. Torrence, CA: Author. For Windows and Mac, this program is excellent for young students and provides wonderful graphics tools for students to create their own images. The program also reads aloud what students have written and allows for the addition of sounds to student work.

Franklyn, Sharon. (1997). *Ultimate Writing and Creativity Center* (Version 1.2) [Computer software]. Cambridge, MA: Softkey Multimedia. A good program for older students which also provides excellent graphics, sound, and composition tools. Includes document layout for newspapers and more.

CHAPTER SEVEN

The Arts Plus = Balance

*Waiting until everything is perfect before making a move is
like waiting to start a trip until all the traffic lights are green.*

—Anonymous

From the other chapters in this book, you know that we consider integration of the arts with other subjects to be essential to the elementary classroom and to learning in general. Numerous examples throughout the book incorporate various features of the arts, including movement and physical education, as they enhance specific subjects. This use provides diverse, multicultural, multisensory, interdisciplinary opportunities to support and enliven your lessons as well as including students who have skill in one or more of the arts. Some chapters conclude with charts containing integrated elements and assessment tips. However, the ideas and examples in this chapter are to be woven into larger content areas; and assessment should be part of that larger context.

The arts are not an add-on or an area to be cut when there are budget problems. Rather, they are an integral part of the development of every young person into a mature learner. Eric Jensen (2001) documents the importance of the arts as a discipline as well as the role the arts play in enhancing the entire curriculum.

According to the *National Standards for Art Education*, established by the U.S. Department of Education, students should know and be able to do the following by the time they have completed secondary school:

- **Communicate at a basic level in the four arts disciplines**—dance, music, theatre, and the visual arts. This includes knowledge and skills in the use of the basic vocabularies, materials, tools, techniques, and intellectual methods of each arts discipline.

- **Communicate proficiently in at least one art form**, including the ability to define and solve artistic problems with insight, reason, and technical proficiency.

- **Develop and present basic analyses of works of art** from structural, historical, and cultural perspectives, and from combinations of those perspectives. This includes the ability to understand and evaluate work in the various arts disciplines.

- **Have an informed acquaintance with exemplary works of art from a variety of cultures and historical periods.** This includes a basic understanding of historical development in the arts disciplines, across the arts as a whole, and within cultures.

- **Relate various types of arts knowledge and skills within and across the arts disciplines.** This includes mixing and matching competencies and understandings in art-making, history and culture, and analysis in any arts-related project.

If you have specialists on your faculty, your class probably participates in regularly scheduled music or art lessons. Students may present special programs, plays, or musical entertainment to parents or a wider community audience. But regardless of those possibilities, your students will be moving toward the fulfillment of the *National Standards* (U.S. Department of Education) when you incorporate the arts into your lessons. As you introduce the arts and keep them before your class, students will make new and exciting connections as creative expression enriches learning.

The elementary classroom offers daily opportunities for exploring one or the other of the arts; and, indeed, those disciplines often parallel, intersect, or cross over as they transform the ordinary into new experiences. The early storyteller-poet was a minstrel who entertained with tales—of travel, adventure, and love—as poems set to music.

For purposes of discussion and example, this chapter will look at each of the arts and consider simple ways you might include them frequently in classroom instruction. Of course, the arts are often practiced as a legitimate discipline or as the center of an important part of the curriculum, particularly in schools where arts specialists, such as music or visual arts teachers, are on staff. This chapter focuses mainly on the integration of the arts into classroom instruction.

INTRODUCING THE VISUAL ARTS

Remember that alphabets began as pictures, and many cultures traditionally combine words and illustrations in finished art. Teachers of all grades can encourage students to draw the pictures that go with their words, whether by hand or on the computer; and when students illustrate their work, the extended thinking is apparent. Alphabet books, counting books, and simple illustrated stories become more sophisticated as students progress through the grades. Those reluctant to draw because of their self-perceived lack of ability should be encouraged to use geometric patterns or designs. Picture books from the library can show students the range of drawing possibilities.

Maintain a picture file and invite students to add to the collection that includes both student artwork and photography. Teachers and students can add to the picture file from old magazines donated to the class. Selections can be used to inspire art as well as stories, so keep them easily available. Crayons, markers, map pencils, chalk, or pastels, as well as pencils and pens, watercolors, and tempera can be used with notebook paper, manila or construction paper, or special art papers. Graphics software helps integrate technology. A butcher's paper mural becomes a class project. Begin with a simple plan and let it grow.

Construct mobiles from string or ribbon, wire, and construction paper. Represent the seasons of the year, the parts of your school or community, the parts of speech, the continents and oceans of the world, Columbus's sailing ships, the solar system—the list goes on, as do the media and techniques that can be used. For example, make the dangling parts from fabric (possibly quilted), Styrofoam, wood, clay, or found materials.

Masks and mask making share a cross-cultural heritage, and students can use them in various ways. Aside from their symbolism, masks will represent characters in nursery rhymes, fairy tales, myths, fables, or adventure stories. They can be drawn or painted—animal, human, or fantastic—on paper or fabric, covering all or part of the face or the entire head. Glitter, feathers, and other ornamentation add color and texture.

Creative expression is an extension of thematic study that works toward a unified concept. This becomes very clear in *Art Express* (Daniel, Hanson, Marstaller, & Monteverde) for kindergarten through Grade 5. Teachers and students alike respond to the simple steps for creating a variety of projects ranging from self-portraits to textile designs, from mosaics to styles of architecture. Sample the wares on the Internet and see examples of student work, keeping in mind that the actual books include outstanding glossaries, printed music for related songs, and numerous adaptable activities.

"And don't forget museum visits and field trips," reminds Susana R. Monteverde, one of the *Art Express* (Daniel et al.) authors and former Curator of Education, Blaffer Gallery, University of Houston, Houston, Texas. "It's very important for students to encounter original works of art. Much like libraries, museums are full of information; and museum educators are very accessible. Tell us what you and your students are about so that we can work with you" (personal communication, September 18, 2001).

INTRODUCING THEATER ARTS

All the world's a stage, and just about everyone enjoys a spot in the limelight now and then. Finger play, pantomime, and readers' theater give an early start to even the youngest learners. Fairy tales and simple stories can be acted out with the teacher narrating while older students write scripts for themselves or for puppet shows.

Storytelling is probably the oldest form of dramatic entertainment, and your students will enjoy telling stories to classmates.

The stories they choose may be old favorites or new pieces specifically written for a particular occasion, such as a historical event, a holiday, or a literature unit. As they rehearse, students should focus first on clear diction and expression. Pacing, too, is important; they should neither rush nor drag through the recitation. With practice and encouragement, your students will acquire poise and assurance as they entertain each other and develop essential speaking skills.

Choral readings adapted from textbooks or favorite poetry collections provide possibilities for group recitation and introduce the class to other speaking opportunities. For example, a narrator or primary reader recites each stanza of a poem with the group responding in chorus (by repeating either a stanza or a single line). Shel Silverstein's books (1974, 1991) are favorites for this kind of material, accessible, easily used, and very engaging for elementary students.

Book reports and other assignments can be written and produced as scripts by older students. Many students don't think of television shows or movies as written work, so here is a chance to emphasize scripts as material written for performance. In so doing, commercials and interviews within the report furnish pertinent information. This simple format can be used for a book report presented as a radio or TV show:

1. Introductory music

2. Interview with a student playing the author of the book

3. Commercial

4. Special musical request from one person to another person

5. Interview with students playing the main characters in the book

6. Closing music

A script for a program like this works for many subjects; the interview might be with a scientist, mathematician, or explorer. You choose. Establish criteria, set up the groups, and show students how to get the information they need; your class, with your help, will take it from there.

Students also will enjoy—and find inspirational—a prop box. Filled with assorted caps and hats, colorful scarves of different sizes, wigs, and eyeglasses, the box will give your class a ready spark to the imagination. For example, a scarf becomes Red Riding Hood's cape, a fortuneteller's shawl, a cowpoke's neckerchief, or a swashbuckler's sash.

Theatrical art comes to life when students experiment and pretend, collaborate and perform. If your circumstance permits, lighting, sets and scenery, costumes, and makeup further contribute to the magic and illusion that is theater.

INTRODUCING MUSIC

Nursery rhymes are often very musical. Counting songs, color songs, and alphabet songs also underscore learning with simple words and tunes. Explore new material as you and your students recast tunes like "Twinkle, Twinkle Little Star" and "Three Blind Mice" with jingles about multiplication tables or spelling words. Move on to new lyrics with other familiar tunes. Using the theme from the *Brady Bunch* television show, for example, Ilona Rosa, third grade teacher in Houston, Texas, wrote "The Turkey Bunch" song, a Thanksgiving ditty performed by her students (see Appendix). Teachers, of course, will know many more; but following are nine examples of nursery rhymes, songs, and popular children's books that serve as the basis for student adaptations: "Humpty-Dumpty," "Old MacDonald," "The Farmer in the Dell," "Here We Go 'Round the Mulberry Bush," "This Old Man," "The Hokey-Pokey," *Brown Bear, Brown Bear, What Do You See?* (Carle & Martin), *Anno's Counting House* (Anno), and *If You Give a Mouse a Cookie* (Bond & Joffe).

Encourage your students to tell stories through music. They might write and sing ballads (four-line stanzas with the rhyme pattern *abcb*) or prepare a very simple script in which all parts are sung (opera). You could stage a work as classroom karaoke in a rousing sing-along that is a popular use of recorded music when songs and studies match.

If you are a musician, share that with your students. Bring the guitar or keyboard; demonstrate on the piano. Show them what is meant by *octave*, and let them hear the notes. Show them written music and play a simple tune. Tell students about your musical work. How did it start? Did you take lessons? How often do you play? Invite students' observations as they listen. If any of your students play instruments, invite them to perform for the class.

Music in the classroom logically opens a wide range of topics related to history, the sciences and development of instruments, or the effect of tone and mood. John Philip Sousa marches mean movement while other selections, such as George Gershwin's *Rhapsody in Blue* and Giacomo Puccini's "Un bel di" from *Madame Butterfly* become the background for periods of sustained silent reading and a way to introduce classical choices. Review the recordings in your school or local library, enjoy them with your class, and find the satisfaction of reaching students through musical expression.

INTRODUCING DANCE AND PHYSICAL EDUCATION

Folk dance, interpretive dance, ballet, gymnastics, and almost any other rhythmic movements allow numerous physical expressions and can become dance in many circumstances. However, where the purist would clearly delineate what constitutes dance, teachers include the larger issue of children's need for physical activity as part of a well-rounded curriculum. Movement, for example, can be used to illustrate or enhance storytelling as well as to mark time in jump rope.

Some schools promote an awareness of the benefits of physical activity by holding health and fitness fairs for students and their families. Such a fair can capitalize on science work in the elementary school or reports students are making on the benefits of exercise and good nutrition. Emphasis can be placed on lifetime sports and activities. These fairs usually involve disseminating information from community groups and health organizations, games, and activities for everyone. Instructional programs might be extended by encouraging evening or weekend activities as homework that supports classroom lessons.

Marcia Shear, physical education teacher at The Fay School in Houston, Texas, frequently collaborates with colleagues to introduce activities that integrate various subjects. For instance, games like ninepins (bowling with empty milk cartons or soda bottles and a playground ball), shooting marbles, playing cup-and-ball games (using whiffle balls attached with string to empty tennis cans), and badminton survive from much earlier times. They not only develop hand-eye coordination but also strengthen ties to social studies.

Nursery rhyme games, bouncing games, circle games, and holiday games can be interspersed throughout the curriculum. Words to "The Farmer in the Dell" can be changed to describe the growth cycle of plants. Hopscotch squares might feature letters rather than numbers, with players supplying words that start with those letters. "The Hokey-Pokey" deals with parts of the body, and so does freeze tag when more scientific terms are used. Tinkertoys sticks or lengths of PVC pipe become rhythm sticks, and so on. "The possibilities are fascinating," says Mrs. Shear, "and encouraging the imagination is extremely important" (personal communication, October 16, 2001).

For older students, Mrs. Shear suggests using balls of different weights and density, as a tie to math and science. Measure and set a course (such as a triangle, rectangle, trapezoid), then observe the differences in performance among a balloon, a marble, a whiffle ball, a golf ball, a baseball, a playground ball. How many strikes or pitches of one ball does it take to play the course as compared with another? Why? Other throwing or tossing games might use a Frisbee, beanbags, or paper airplanes.

"Basic games equipment for the classroom teacher should be inexpensive and space-efficient," says Mrs. Shear. "Ideally, everything would fit inside a 12-inch-square milk crate" (personal communication, October 16, 2001). The list might include

- A playground ball
- Ropes of different lengths (to use in tug-of-war and for jumping rope)
- Bandannas (to use in games needing flags and in circle games, to use as blindfolds, and for dividing teams by color)
- Marbles
- Balloons and string (to play indoor court games, even with a net between two chairs)
- Empty soda bottles (to use as markers and cones)
- Bean bags (to use in relay or tossing games)
- Chalk

"With these basics, the classroom teacher can help students develop balance, coordination, and rhythm," says Mrs. Shear. "And this serves very well the fact that the body naturally moves in a rhythmical manner" (personal communication, October 16, 2001).

All forms of dance and physical activity are related to health. Eliminating or reducing physical education from the curriculum is a bad idea in a society where poor conditioning and obesity are pervasive and persistent problems.

SUMMARY

The arts remain an integral part of the elementary curriculum, both in their own right and as a part of the rest of the curriculum. Students of all ages benefit from the visual arts, theater, music, dance, and physical education. Personal expression in every form enriches learning in the various content areas.

RESOURCES

Anno, Mitsumasa. (1992). *Anno's Counting House*. New York: HarperCollins Juvenile Books.

Bond, Felicia, & Joffe, Laura. (1985). *If You Give a Mouse a Cookie*. New York: HarperCollins Juvenile Books.

Carle, Eric, & Martin, Bill, Jr. (1992). *Brown Bear, Brown Bear, What Do You See?* New York: Henry Holt.

Daniel, Vesta, Hanson, Lee, Marstaller, Kristen Pederson, & Monteverde, Susana R. (1998). *Art Express, Grades K-5*. Orlando, FL: Harcourt Brace.

Jensen, Eric. (2001). *Arts With the Brain in Mind*. Alexandria, VA: Association for Supervision and Curriculum Development.

Silverstein, Shel. (1974). *Where the Sidewalk Ends*. New York: HarperCollins Juvenile Books.

Silverstein, Shel. (1991). *A Light in the Attic*. New York: Knopf.

U.S. Department of Education. (n.d.). *National Standards for Art Education*. Retrieved July 30, 2002, from www.ed.gov/pubs/ArtsStandards.html

Web Sites

"Songs of the Century." A project to promote better understanding of America's musical and cultural heritage; an initiative for schools through the National Endowment for the Arts, the Recording Industry Association of America, Scholastic Inc., and AOL@SCHOOL. Retrieved July 30, 2002, from www.arts.gov/endownews/news01/songs.html

Songs of the 50s and 60s. Lyrics. Retrieved July 30, 2002, from www.crystal-reflections.com/songs/songs.htm

Songs from the 40s through the 70s. Lyrics. Retrieved July 30, 2002, from www.rockinwoman.com

Sites for Lesson Plans

A to Z Teacher Stuff, L.L.C. Retrieved July 30, 2002, from www.atozteacherstuff.com/themes

American Red Cross Water Safety Programs. Retrieved July 30, 2002, from www.redcross.org

AOL at School. Retrieved July 30, 2002, from www.school.aol.com

Education World. Retrieved July 30, 2002, from www.educationworld.com

Harcourt Brace educational site. Retrieved July 30, 2002, from www.harcourtschool.com

J. Paul Getty Trust. Retrieved July 30, 2002, from www.getty.edu/artsednet

Jump Rope for Heart Program. Retrieved July 30, 2002, from www.americanheart.org

National Endowment for the Arts. Retrieved July 30, 2002, from www.arts.gov

Scholastic, Inc. Retrieved July 30, 2002, from www.scholastic.com

CHAPTER EIGHT

Literacy and the Library Media Center

The library deeps lay waiting for them.

—Ray Bradbury (1998, p. 13)

Literacy is the result of language development and is more than the sum of its parts—reading, writing, listening, and speaking. Fluent language is rooted in practice; and like those of any other achievement, the basic skills require use. This chapter, therefore, explores the relationship between the classroom teacher and the school librarian or library media specialist as together they work with students in this effort. While not all schools have a librarian, the chapter contains much useful information and many suggestions that easily can be adapted to circumstance. Whether you work with a school librarian, public librarian, or with other colleagues, consider ways to enlist reading coaches, mentors, and other volunteers as language development becomes a rich and challenging experience for your students.

The skills and methods involved in successful reading programs, discussed in Chapter 2, are well-known to the vast majority of elementary teachers. However, the American Association of School

Librarians (1999, retrieved August 1, 2002, from www.ala.org/aasl/positions) underscores the importance of schoolwide emphasis concerning the following elements considered integral to an effective reading (language development) program:

- The library media center is flexibly scheduled so that students and teachers have unlimited physical and intellectual access to a wide range of materials. Students are not limited to using only commercially prescribed or teacher-selected materials.
- Students choose from a varied, non-graded collection of materials which reflect their personal interests.
- Students learn to identify, analyze, and synthesize information by using a variety of materials in a variety of formats.
- Multidisciplinary approaches to teaching and learning are encouraged.
- Teachers and library media specialists cooperatively select materials and collaboratively plan activities that offer students an integrated approach to learning.
- Teachers and library media specialists share responsibility for reading and information literacy instruction. They plan and teach collaboratively, based on the needs of the student.
- Continual staff development is critical to reading instruction.

With the librarian or library media specialist involved in the transition from the textbook-centered classroom to the resource-based library media center, students learn *how to learn* through the process of learning itself. They discover how knowledge is organized and learn to find and use information. They practice literacy.

Regardless of your instructional program, the school librarian and library media center are central in developing literacy skills. As the campus expert in information location and management, the librarian's role is rich and versatile and enhances the language development program through the following characteristics:

Characteristic 1: Ability to identify and select age-appropriate and curriculum-specific literature

Characteristic 2: Ability to provide reading opportunities

Characteristic 3: Ability to maintain organization of resources

Characteristic 4: Ability to direct and implement the purchase of materials

Characteristic 5: Ability to devise strategies for computer-based data and information seeking

CHARACTERISTIC 1: ABILITY TO IDENTIFY AND SELECT AGE-APPROPRIATE AND CURRICULUM-SPECIFIC LITERATURE

Working with the classroom teacher, the school librarian will recommend interest- and curriculum-specific materials as well as materials at the appropriate reading level for the individual student or class. Even for young students in a prereading stage, the librarian may suggest specific, computer-based programs, videos, tapes, and books.

At all grade levels, the school librarian helps teachers to develop thematic units. Librarians assist in securing lists of community speakers and special visitors, field trip locations, and names of resource persons in specialized areas. The librarian helps teachers to understand that technology is a tool for obtaining and reporting knowledge. Of course, constantly revising the list of good literature available to students is a central part of the librarian's work.

In tandem with the classroom teacher, the school librarian will emphasize the enduring qualities of good literature. Good literature offers a powerful story, rich language, memorable characters, and lessons that remain with us. Good literature includes stories read and enjoyed by generations, interesting to adults as well as children, and frequently based on strong ideals.

Some primary grade (K-3) classics include *Aesop for Children* (Winter & Winter), the fairy tales of Hans Christian Andersen, Ludwig Bemelmans's *Madeline* books, and *When We Were Very Young* and *Winnie the Pooh* by A. A. Milne. Intermediate grade suggestions include *Johnny Tremaine* by Esther Forbes, *The Wind in the Willows* by Kenneth Grahame, *Greek Myths* by Ingri D'Aulaire and Edgar Parin, and *Tales From Shakespeare* by Charles Lamb and Mary Lamb. See Box 8.1 for additional suggestions.

Of course, this is just a beginning list, not to mention that preferences will vary from school to school. Book lists at grade level are

(text continues on page 132)

Box 8.1   Recommended Reading

K-1
Read-Aloud Books
A Is for Africa by Ifeoma Onyefulu, and other alphabet books
Danny and the Dinosaur by Syd Hoff
Little Bear books by E. H. Minarik
Tales of Peter Rabbit and His Friends by Beatrix Potter
Yeh-Shen: A Cinderella Story From China by Ai-Ling Louie
Greek Myths by Ingri D'Aulaire and Edgar Parin
And other fables, fairy tales, and legends from various
    countries and cultures.

2
American Tall Tales by Mary Pope Osborne
American Tall Tales by Adrien Stoutenburg
Arthur (I Can Read series) by Lillian Hoban
Paul Bunyan, A Tall Tale by Steve Kellogg
Pecos Bill by Sarah Kilbourne
The Emperor's New Clothes by Han Christian Andersen
The Night Has Ears: African Proverbs by Ashley Bryan

3
Anansi Does the Impossible! An Ashanti Tale by Verna
    Aardman
Androcles and the Lion: An Aesop Fable by Janet Stevens
And biographies of famous explorers and scientists drawn
    from students' social studies and science textbooks.
Chapter books to extend classroom studies
Dragon and the Wicked Knight by Ogden Nash
Gods and Goddesses of the Ancient Norse by L. E. Fisher
Greek Myths by Olivia Collidge
Little House series by Laura Ingalls Wilder
Poems by Lewis Carroll
Ramona by Beverly Cleary
Roman Myths by Geraldine McCaughrean
And poems by Ogden Nash

(Continued)

Box 8.1 Continued

4

Famous Illustrated Speeches and Documents, a series from
　　ABDO Publishing
From Daybreak to Good Night: Poems for Children by Carl
　　Sandburg
Gulliver's Travels by Jonathan Swift
Junebug by Alice Mead
King Arthur and the Knights of the Round Table by Howard
　　Pyle
And nonfiction prose to extend classroom studies

5

*Abraham Lincoln's Gettysburg Address: Four Score and
　　More* by Barbara S. Feinberg
Sherlock Holmes by Arthur Conan Doyle
"The Battle Hymn of the Republic" by Julia Ward Howe
The Gettysburg Address by Abraham Lincoln
The Legend of Scarface: A Blackfeet Indian Tale by Robert D. San
　　Souci
The Songs My Paddle Sings: Native American Legends by
　　James Riordan
And other mystery stories

6

Roll of Thunder, Hear My Cry by Mildred Taylor
Story of Pygmalion by Pamela Espeland
The Faber Book of Greek Legends edited by Kathleen Lines
The House on Mango Street by Sandra Cisneros
The Secret Garden by Frances Hodgson Burnett
And poems by Rudyard Kipling, Edgar Allen Poe, and Henry
　　Wadsworth Longfellow

---

available from many libraries and associations. Consult your
school librarian or library media specialist regarding particular
needs, or request from this person lists published by the following:

- Newbery Medal Award Books
- Caldecott Medal Award Books
- H. C. Andersen International Books
- Young Reader's Choice Award List
- Science Fiction and Fantasy for Children (compiled by Linda Day)

When students write and use the library media center to extend their research (especially in the case of intermediate or upper elementary grades), the school librarian may assist teachers in developing criteria for use in evaluating finished work. For example, a checklist might include basic points of information gathering: Has the student used Internet sites? Has the student gone to the shelves to pull books or made use of periodicals? As part of the literacy team, the librarian evaluates how well students understand and apply their skills.

CHARACTERISTIC 2: ABILITY TO PROVIDE READING OPPORTUNITIES

An appealing setting stimulates curiosity, creativity, and exploration. The school library can provide space for young people to think and reflect; space for a student pair to discuss, revise, and edit their work; space for small groups to meet with the librarian; or space for a teacher or librarian to direct a larger group. Here, too, the school librarian coordinates the activities of volunteers who help out in the library media center, assist with the book fair, or visit as guest speakers, readers, or storytellers. Beanbag chairs and a rocking chair coexist with the small tiered reading arena-theater or elementary chairs and tables and the latest technology the school can afford.

The school librarian exercises vital support by assisting teachers to connect reading and writing as their comprehension of literacy deepens and to implement the right strategies for individual students. Examples include frequent reading aloud, finding the means to teach reading through both systematic phonics and literature, and devising home reading lists. The librarian also may introduce students to libraries outside the school such as law or medical libraries, health and science libraries, presidential libraries, those on the campuses of colleges or universities, local public libraries, or libraries associated with special community interests, such as heritage museums.

Students need many opportunities to read aloud in their development of overall language and literacy skills, whether reading for information or personal pleasure. Modeling good reading habits should begin as early as possible. Working individually, with small groups or with a whole class, the librarian should set up centers that provide a setting for all to read simultaneously, either silently or aloud. Students can browse and sample books, magazines, pamphlets, newspapers, CDs, and tapes. By moving beyond the textbook, these sessions stimulate interest in reading and literary appreciation. Here, again, cooperation between teacher and librarian regarding individual reading levels provides developmental support.

As students develop literacy skills, they should be taught the following, using the library:

- To locate the information required for their assignments (by starting with the card or computer catalog and encyclopedias)
- To evaluate that information within the framework of the assignment (by making sure the student understands the scope of the assignment)
- To synthesize the information by reducing it to its essential elements and adapting it to the new purpose (by summarizing and paraphrasing the most important points and beginning the written work within a new context)
- To integrate the information and new knowledge (by starting with what the student knows about the topic and adding to it in a logical manner)
- To apply the new knowledge as required (by using it)

The school librarian also will demonstrate how to access materials and Web sites that extend and enhance the curriculum or assignment. Location skills in the library media center are important to all students—from gifted students to those who may need information in a different language; to students whose interests are as different as dinosaurs, mythology, or Shakespeare. Each of these students needs to know how to find and get information.

Students with learning differences also find success with the help of the library media specialist by locating and using multimedia sources, both print and nonprint, technology and CDs, visuals and videos. By incorporating other disciplines such as art or music, and with the assistance of the librarian, the classroom teacher can enlist the expertise of other specialists in the building.

CHARACTERISTIC 3: ABILITY TO MAINTAIN ORGANIZATION OF RESOURCES

A good library media center should have open access; it is available to students and teachers throughout the school day. Ideally, most students and teachers are well prepared to use the library, so the librarian is not overwhelmed. This happens when the library media specialist has done an excellent job in preparing students and teachers to access information.

The librarian also teaches information skill gathering, so these skills can be integrated into a literature-based curriculum. As soon as students are able to read and begin to understand different organizational systems, such as alphabetical or numerical, they also see how these apply to the library.

Specific book information (formerly found in the card catalog, now often computer based) includes the author, book title, location of the book on the shelf, publisher, date and place of publication, a short summary of the book, and references to related subjects and materials. The librarian also will introduce students to standard reference materials—dictionaries, encyclopedias, atlases, indexes—and to periodicals such as newspapers, magazines, and journals. Library media centers often maintain a picture file stocked with photographs, charts, and maps organized for access and availability. Students should be introduced to this material as well as computer sites for such material.

See Box 8.2 for some of the skills, by grade, that should be reinforced in the library.

In addition, an introduction to technology must address questions such as, How are the computers set up? Who has access to the computers and under what circumstances? Does the school have a technology policy manual? Students must know if their library has electronic access to other libraries, within this system

(text continues on page 137)

Box 8.2   Skills Students Learn in the Library

K

Learn basic terms such as *author* and *illustrator*.
Learn basic story parts: title, beginning, end.
Demonstrate using *Mother Goose* poems.

1

Learn basic terms such as *character, hero, heroine*.
Demonstrate using simple stories, beginning reader books.

2

Identify myth, limerick.
Tell and write their own stories.
Demonstrate with accounts of real-life heroes.

3

Identify and find biography, autobiography, fiction,
    nonfiction, dictionary, table of contents.

4

Identify characteristics of the novel and short story: plot,
    setting.
Identify purpose and audience of the work; use
    encyclopedias, magazines.
Learn to document sources in beginning bibliographies.

5

Learn dramatic terms and characteristics such as *comedy,
    tragedy, act, scene*.
Document sources in a simple bibliography.

6

Learn literary terms and devices such as *epic, imagery,
    symbol, personification*.
Learn the elements of a brief research essay: Gather
    information, take notes, organize outline, prepare
    bibliography.

(to another school perhaps) or outside this system (restricted to another library system or to the greater world at large through the Internet).

Regardless of age, the acquisition of knowledge is developmental. The librarian should guide the classroom teacher in appropriate measures by grade level so that when a student leaves sixth grade, all of these skills are in place.

CHARACTERISTIC 4: ABILITY TO DIRECT AND IMPLEMENT THE PURCHASE OF MATERIALS

The school librarian or library media specialist should take a leadership role in organizing a team or committee of teachers, parents, administrators, and interested community members to recommend areas that need to be strengthened and to review materials and purchases. With various groups and views represented, decisions are more soundly based; and the librarian is able to make excellent purchases with limited funds. Library media center committees and purchases often lead to other services and developments.

The formation of multilevel student reading clubs frequently leads to the expansion of a particular collection as students pursue a growing interest. Biographies and other nonfiction often spur reading among elementary students. Upper elementary students especially are impressed with keeping track of the number of books—sometimes even the number of pages—they read, and are proud to keep records over the course of a school year. Tracking the books and pages read integrates with other curriculum content areas when students construct line, circle, or bar graphs in math; when time lines and historical and other settings are correlated with social studies; and when classification and categorization of information can be applied to science.

Regarding revenue, the annual book fair is a popular means of building library funds. Some publishers maintain book fair divisions to assist schools; some local bookstores sponsor events. Many schools encourage students or their families to donate a book to the library to mark a birthday or other special occasion. And the library fund remains popular with parents and grandparents who make school contributions. The library, and events and activities associated with the library, support students' delight in discovery, encouraging enthusiasm and success in learning. Keeping families interested in student well-being and school events garners support for the school system.

CHARACTERISTIC 5: ABILITY TO DEVISE STRATEGIES FOR COMPUTER-BASED DATA AND INFORMATION SEEKING

The appropriate use of technology for research, whether on the Internet or through CDs or online databases, is to gather, select, synthesize, and evaluate relevant information. In concert with the classroom teacher, the school librarian provides relevant, meaningful instruction; assists in teaching students to apply information to problem solving; and encourages the production of appropriate student work. Summary, interpretation, and attribution of information must be emphasized. These would be important under any circumstance; they become even more significant when students have access to information via technology. With the librarian's assistance, or that of the technology specialist, students should be given opportunities to do the following:

1. Develop basic keyboarding skills that avoid hunt-and-peck, and learn to use important keys such as tab, shift, and punctuation marks

2. Learn to use available word processing software to compose short sentences and, eventually, a short essay

3. Practice editing skills using cut and paste functions in their software

4. Use CD-ROMs and computerized card catalogs and encyclopedias to locate specific information

5. Learn terms pertinent to Internet research such as *URL, Web site,* and *search engine*

6. Perform research using search engines to locate relevant material (for example, using "Aesop's Fables" as the key

words, students can browse hundreds of fables, choose among them, and print according to criteria set by the teacher).

The librarian, often with a committee of teachers and a district technology specialist, can set up a relatively simple training program to ensure that students learn new computer possibilities each year that will help them with their work. For more information regarding the integration of technology in the elementary classroom, see Chapter 6.

SUMMARY

As the availability of information expands, so does the role of the school library media specialist. With the ability to identify and choose literature, to provide reading opportunities, to organize resources, to select materials for permanent collections, and to develop strategies for collecting computer-based data, the resident wizard in your library media center is invaluable.

RESOURCES

Aardman, Aaredma, Verna. (1997). *Anansi Does the Impossible! An Ashanti Tale.* New York: Atheneum.

ABDO Publishing. Series of *Famous Illustrated Speeches and Documents.* Edina, MN: Author. Retrieved August 7, 2002, from www.abdopub.com/c/@6DOrsc.DCBByw/Pages/product.html?record@P168

American Association of School Librarians. (1999). *Position Statement on Resource Based Instruction: Role of the School Library Media Specialist in Reading Development* (Rev. ed.). Retrieved August 1, 2002, from www.ala.org/aasl/positions

Andersen, Hans Christian (2000). *The Emperor's New Clothes.* Cambridge, MA: Candlewick Press.

Bemelmans, Ludwig. (1939). *Madeline.* New York: Simon & Schuster. All the books in the Madeline series make good reading.

Bradbury, Ray. (1998). *Something Wicked This Way Comes.* New York: Avon.

Bryan, Ashley. (1999). *The Night Has Ears: African Proverbs.* New York: Atheneum.

Burnett, France Hodgson. (1994). *The Secret Garden.* New York: Barnes & Noble. (Original work published in 1911.) Available free online: retrieved August 7, 2002, from etext.lib.virginia.edu/toc/modeng/public/BurSecr.html

Carroll, Lewis. (1973). *Poems.* New York: Harper Collins.

Cisneros, Sandra. (1984). *The House on Mango Street.* New York: Vintage.

Cleary, Beverly. (1992). *Ramona.* New York: Morrow.

Collidge, Olivia. (2001). *Greek Myths.* Boston: Houghton Mifflin.

D'Aulaire, Ingri, & Parin, Edgar. (1962). *Greek Myths.* New York: Doubleday.

Doyle, Arthur Conan. (2002). *Sherlock Holmes.* Edina, MN: ABDO Publishing.

Espeland, Pamela. (1981). *Story of Pygmalion.* Minneapolis, MN: Learner Publishing Group.

Feinberg, Barbara S. (2000). *Abraham Lincoln's Gettysburg Address: Four Score and More.* Brookfield, CT: Millbrook Press.

Fisher, Leonard Everett. (2001). *Gods and Goddesses of the Ancient Norse.* New York: Holiday House.

Forbes, Esther. (1986). *Johnny Tremaine.* New York: Dell.

Grahame, Kenneth. (1954). *The Wind in the Willows.* New York: Scribner.

Gunning, Thomas G. (2000). *Best Books for Building Literacy for Elementary School Children.* Boston: Allyn & Bacon.

Hirsch, E. Donald, Jr. (Ed.). (1999). *Core Knowledge Series.* Charlottesville, VA: Core Knowledge Foundation. Seven volumes, organized one per grade, beginning with *What Your Kindergartner Needs to Know,* ending with *What Your Sixth Grader Needs to Know.*

Hoban, Lillian. (1982). *Arthur* (I Can Read series). New York: Harper Collins.

Hoff, Syd (1978). *Danny and the Dinosaur* (I Can Read series). New York: Harper Collins.

Kellogg, Steve. (1985). *Paul Bunyan, A Tall Tale.* New York: Morrow.

Kilbourne, Sarah. (1992). *Pecos Bill.* New York: Morrow.

Lamb, Charles, & Lamb, Mary. (1988). *Tales From Shakespeare.* New York: Penguin Putnam.

Lincoln, Abraham. (1998). *The Gettysburg Address.* Boston: Houghton Mifflin.

Lines, Kathleen. (Ed.). (1986). *The Faber Book of Greek Legends.* London: Faber & Faber.

Louie, Ai-Ling. (1982). *Yeh-Shen: A Cinderella Story From China.* Kirkwood, NY: Philomel.

McCaughrean, Geraldine. (2001). *Roman Myths.* New York: Simon & Schuster.

Mead, Alice. (1995). *Junebug.* Scranton, PA: HarperCollins.

Milne, A. A. (1939). *When We Were Very Young.* New York: Dutton.

Milne, A. A. (1956). *Winnie the Pooh.* New York: Dutton. (Original work published in 1926.)

Minarik, Else H. (1976). *Little Bear* (I Can Read series). New York: Harper Collins.

Nash, Ogden. (1999). *Dragon and the Wicked Knight.* Boston: Little, Brown.

Onyefulu, Ifeoma. (1993). *A Is for Africa.* Bergenfield, NJ: Penguin.

Osborne, Mary Pope. (1991). *American Tall Tales.* New York: Knopf.

Potter, Beatrix. (1984). *Tales of Peter Rabbit and His Friends.* New York: Random House.

Pyle, Howard. (2002). *King Arthur and the Knights of the Round Table.* Edina, MN: ABDO Publishing.

Riordan, James. (1997). *The Song My Paddle Sings: Native American Legends.* Salisbury Mills, NY: Pavilion Books.

Sandburg, Carl. (2001). *From Daybreak to Good Night: Poems for Children.* Toronto, ON, Canada: Annick Press.

Sans Souci, Robert D. (1996). *The Legend of Scarface: A Blackfeet Indian Tale.* New York: Bantam Doubleday Dell.

Sierra, Judy. (2002). *Can You Guess My Name? Traditional Tales Around the World.* New York: Houghton Mifflin.

Stevens, Janet. (1989). *Androcles and the Lion: An Aesop Fable.* New York: Holiday House.

Stoutenburg, Adrien. (1996). *American Tall Tales.* Bergenfield, NJ: Penguin Putnam.

Swift, Jonathan. (2002). *Gulliver's Travels* (adaptations). Edina, MN: ABDO Publishing.

Taylor, Mildred. (1997). *Roll of Thunder, Hear My Cry.* Bergenfield, NJ: Puffin.

Wilder, Laura Ingalls. (1989). *Little House* series. New York: Harper Trophy.

Winter, Mio, & Winter, Milo. (1994) *The Aesop for Children.* New York: Scholastic Trade.

Web Sites

American Library Association. Retrieved August 1, 2002, from www.ala.org

Children's Book Links. Retrieved August 1, 2002, from www.absolutesway.com/pfp/html/childrens.htm

Children's Literature Web Guide. Retrieved August 1, 2002, from www.acs.ucalgary.ca/~dkbrown/index.html

Core Knowledge Foundation. Retrieved August 1, 2002, from www.coreknowledge.org

Hans Christian Andersen. Retrieved August 1, 2002, from www.hca.gilead.org.il

Howe, Julia Ward. (1862). "The Battle Hymn of the Republic." Retrieved August 9, 2002, from www.nationalcenter. org/BattleHymnoftheRepublic.html

Learning to Read; Resources for Language Arts and Reading Research. Retrieved August 1, 2002, from www.toread.com

Newbery Library. Retrieved August 1, 2002 from http://library. thinkquest.org/J001456

CHAPTER NINE

In Conclusion

*What is required is sight and insight—then you might add
one more: excite.*

—Robert Frost (n.d.)

Fundamental to this book is the understanding that sound
teaching principles rely more on methods than on particular materials. Methods are applied to the high-quality materials
selected by teachers and administrators. Accountability, then, is
grounded in excellent curriculum, effective teaching, and interested participants whose test scores and other important assessments reflect achievement.

Like other professions, education is rife with jargon and
acronyms and phrases—diversity, multicultural, interdisciplinary,
multi-sensory, block scheduling, multiple intelligences, individualized education program plan (IEP), English as a second language
(ESL), limited English proficiency (LEP), and others—words and
phrases not always fully clarified. In this book, we have tried very
hard to use plain English and to show the meaning of methods we
recommend.

What we have learned from the methods we present is that all
students learn more effectively when the elements of such methods
are applied across the curriculum. In this book we have, therefore,
suggested ways to make learning more effective, more engaging,
and more satisfying and lasting for both teacher and student—by
offering many ways to revamp and integrate curriculum.

With the concepts presented here, teachers can expand and enhance their art, and students can become enthusiastic learners. Schools become not hierarchies of bureaucracy but communities of learning involving administrators, teachers, students, parents, and the larger community. Each chapter of this book presents a content area, not with specific textbooks or materials in mind but with ways to approach whichever materials a teacher chooses or uses as part of an established curriculum. In this fashion, the elements under discussion are viewed and presented as applicable to any program or set of materials a teacher or school might choose. You can, therefore, use this book comprehensively or chapter by chapter to examine one or two or three specific areas of the curriculum.

As your experience grows to include a widening range of colleagues and collaborations, so will your sense of enthusiasm and invigoration. You will have come full circle with the reasons you chose the profession. Whether you are working alone or working with colleagues, the effort will infuse your teaching and transfer to your students. And that enthusiasm for growth and learning is the point of our profession as we strive to spark the flame of learning.

RESOURCE

Frost, Robert. (n.d.). Retrieved July 31, 2002, from www.chesco.com~artman/frost.html

Appendix

Following are assessment examples, poems, and pictures referenced in the book, which teachers may find helpful. Please see Table A.1 for a guide to the chapters where items in this Appendix are mentioned.

Table A.1   Key to Chapters Where Appendix Contents Are Mentioned

Title of Appendix Item	*Chapters*
1. Writing Final Assessment	2
2. Critics' Choice	2, 3, 4
3. Formula Poem	6
4. Insect Drawing and Labeling	6
5. "Turkey Bunch" Song	7

WRITING FINAL ASSESSMENT

Note: This sixth-grade essay by Peter Boedeker is an example of self-assessment. It has been copied as submitted for scoring. The teacher was able to score for content, mechanics, and conventional usage while learning about the student's experience. The essay follows the directions as they were given to the class. Following are the instructions the students were given.

Using Your Skills

We have studied and discussed many readings since the beginning of the semester. We then used those as the basis for our writing assignments. Now use the following directions to write an essay at least three paragraphs long.

Think back over your work in this class. Choose the assignment you most enjoyed. Write about that assignment. Develop your paragraphs with supporting details and examples.

In the first paragraph, discuss the assignment. (For example, what was the assignment? Why did you enjoy it? What did you learn?) In the second paragraph, discuss the study skills needed to complete the assignment. In the third paragraph, discuss how these skills have helped you, even perhaps, in another class.

You are free to use your class notes, to color code your preliminary work (including lists or rough draft), and to use the dictionary. Your rough draft and finished essay are due at the end of the period.

Peter Boedeker

Writing, 6

May 18, 2000

Writing Final

One of the best assignments that my class took, I think, was the poem. This particular poem instructed us to write about a color and put it in a poem format. I liked this task because it was something new that I had not done before. I learned that a poem starts with capital letters on each line, has basically the same punctuation as any other written work, like commas and periods, and that a poem's lines are set up differently than our other assignments.

There were three main study skills involved in writing the poem. The first that we had to know was the format and how to set it up. Secondly, the class had to understand and follow the set list of directions. Lastly, we needed to use are imagination to come up with the colors that related to our chosen one. These are the study skills that were needed for this assignment.

The skills above have also helped me develope in my other subjects. Knowing how the format works allows me to differentiate the poem from normal stories that are in paragraph form. Following directions has helped me in all of my classes because I now analyze my instructions very closely to not make any mistakes. Using my imagination has inabled me to really get into the stories that we read and make me feel like I'm part of the action, like in King Arthur. These are all the things I enjoyed about writing the poem.

THE CRITICS' CHOICE

E*valu*ation (root word = *value*, i.e., of worth or importance) takes time and reflection. Students in Sandra Johnston's first-grade class at MacArthur Elementary School, Houston, Texas, considered three writing lessons. Volunteers stated each lesson in a sentence, and the group revised until we had these statements on the board:

We used our five senses to write music.

We used the shape of a number to draw a picture.

We described things that were red and wrote a poem.

After review and discussion, these directions were written on the board:

1. Choose your favorite lesson.

2. Why was this your favorite?

3. Write sentences about the lesson.

4. Draw your picture to match the writing.

Here are some of the students' responses:

We used our five senses
because it wus fun. and we lisind. and we
got it all rite. and the nexd day
we got it rite agen.

—Germiah May

We used the shape of a number to draw a picture.
I had more fun. It was fun because we where drowing
picture. I like to drow because it helps me tink.

—Paige Watts

I like the five senses. It was my favorite because I said init was warm
cocoa and I like warm cocoa and I left warm cocoa for Santa Clus.

snow winter ice snowball house
skate friend six blanket cold

—Aaron Ghazy

My favorite lesson is when we used our five sense to write to music
because it made me feel like I am in the music and I was dancing to it.
And I used my amagunasion.

—Maggie Lozano

We described things that were red and wrote a poem.
Because we no what kind of things are red. We described the color
red because we want to think about a red color. And we had think
about it. And I emajend in my mind. And we had close our eyes and
I lesson to the story.

—Xiaoqing Dui

I like the one when we used our five senses to write
to music because It looked like I was going to heaven
because
I used my
Amaganation.
god rolled
from the
dead on the
third day.

—Marvin Sims

My favorite is went I used our five senses.
Because I have write a pome with
musuk. and I like to write musck

—Sirena Pena

yuesing the five senses because
It is ixcititeng because of the words
we wrote.

—Terrell Cloud

I like the red Hot because the volcano is red Hot.
I will write about the three volcanos. They are red
Hot and Hot to doystoy the villige.
Shoots up in the air.

—Kevin Hawkins

My favrite is when we used our five senses to write to the
music because we wrote the five sentences and we wrote a poem.

—Shamiah Davenport

I like when we used our five senses to write to music.
Because we had closd our eyes and think about smlling eating
hereing and tuching. I liked it about an angol eating
in my amgnshun at a reshron. It was eating yummy
shrip.

—Jacob Figueroa

FORMULA POEM

Figure A.1   By Michaela Hollo, Fifth Grade, The Fay School,
                 Houston, Texas

Michaela
Smart, funny
Rides like the wind
Hoping to be an olympic horseback rider one day
Hollo

INSECT DRAWING AND LABELING

Figure A.2 By Bradley Berry, Second Grade, The Fay School, Houston, Texas

This is a Tsetse fly.

"TURKEY BUNCH" SONG

"The Turkey Bunch" by Ilona Rosa

Sung to theme from the *Brady Bunch* television show:

This is a story about a holiday
That was started a long, long time ago,
When the Mayflower brought the Pilgrims,
In 1620 or so.

And when the Pilgrims landed in Plymouth,
Life was very difficult, you see.
They didn't have much food or winter clothing;
Help was needed desperately.

Until one day when the Pilgrims met the Indians,
And they knew that it was much more than a lunch,
That this group would somehow form a colony;
That's the way they all became the Turkey Bunch.

The Turkey Bunch,
The Turkey Bunch,
That's the way they became
The Turkey Bunch.

Index